THE MYSTERIES OF KIN

King's College Chapel is one of the and its world-famous pinnacles dominate the Cambridge skyline. In this absorbing study the author describes the occult principles on which the chapel was built, revealing that it has never been used for the purpose intended by its founder, the saintly King Henry VI.

NIGEL PENNICK 1973·181·

THE MYSTERIES OF KING'S COLLEGE CHAPEL

by

NIGEL PENNICK

AQUARIAN

THE AQUARIAN PRESS
Wellingborough, Northamptonshire

First published 1974
This edition 1978
Second impression (under Aquarian Press imprint) 1982

ISBN 0 85030 331 1

Printed and bound in Great Britain

Acknowledgements

Various parts of this book have appeared previously as my articles in *Arcana* and *The Oracle of Albion*. I thank the editors of these magazines for permission to republish this material. I would also like to thank the staff of Cambridge Reference Library for assistance in my researches, especially the Staff of the Cambridgeshire Collection.

*Quod superius est sicut quod inferius,
et quod inferius est sicut quod superius
ad perpentranda miracula rei unuis.*
Hermes Trismegistus

Contents

Introduction

The Chapel of King's College of Our Lady and St. Nicholas in Cambridge is as synonymous with Cambridge in the popular imagination as the Eiffel tower with Paris or the pyramids with Egypt. Almost any publication, from the telephone directory upwards, dealing with Cambridge, is illustrated by one view or another of King's College Chapel. Undoubtedly, it is the most photographed building in the city, being recorded on film by the thousands of visitors who daily stream thru its Gothic portals. In its commanding position on King's Parade, the former High Street, King's College Chapel can be seen from many parts of the town, unobscured by tower blocks, which are banned in Cambridge. To the tourists who 'do' the chapel as if a duty, it is merely an art gallery in which to stare at *"The Adoration of the Magi"*, a 1634 painting by Rubens (defaced in 1974), and in which to buy guide-books, records and tea-towels.

The chapel has, in its long history, been spared the iconoclastic blows of the Puritan maniac William Dowsing, been lambasted in print by the 'Aesthetic' Ruskin, and in this, a supposedly enlightened century, desecrated by a costly Rubens which was never intended to be in King's College Chapel, idolatrously replacing the high-altar cross. Even before it reached its present sorry state, the religious spirit and geomantic truth was perverted, firstly by King Henry VII's temporal heraldic.

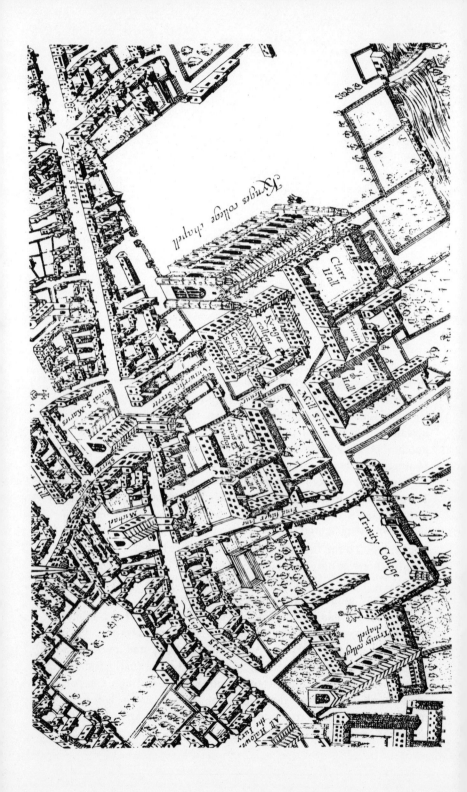

impress, then by the imported alien art of Henry VIII, the notorious Tudor tyrant.

Surprisingly, in the textbooks of Gothic Architecture, King's College Chapel receives much less attention than it deserves, despite its uniqueness, having the widest fan-vaulting anywhere in existence, and the finest windows of painted glass surviving in England.

The official guide-books themselves fail in giving but one part of the story, whilst quoting how many tons of water from tourists' breath the walls absorb per annum, the other side is forgotten or ignored. To quote Aldous Huxley *"Facts do not cease to exist because they are ignored."* The mechanistic side is dealt with, but the religious and occult side is never even hinted at. No book prior to this study has even attempted to touch upon the occult treasury which is the Church of Our Lady and Saint Nicholas in Cambridge.

1

The Background

Cambridge has been for millennia an important religious centre. Wandlebury, to the South, was, during Celtic times, the central shrine of the area, sacred to the Mother Goddess Gogmagog, with the chalk-cut effigies of Gog, Magog and Wandil, visited, legend has it, by Boudicca and her Iceni army on their way to fight against the usurping Roman tyranny.

Of Durolipons, the Roman city made from the British Caer Gwrgan, little is known of religious connexions, excepting that the present church of St. Peter, off Castle Street, stands on the site of the Temple of Diana. After the withdrawal of the Roman legions and the death of King Arthur, the city was abandoned.

In the mystico-defensive island of the Armeswerk was discovered, by miraculous revelation, the splendid marble coffin which was to hold the mortal remains of Aethelthryth (St. Etheldreda), foundress of the Abbey of Ely. The nuns had sailed along the River Granta from Ely to the Armeswerk, which included the present site of Magdalene College. It was separated on the south of the river, and on the north by the "Watercourse called Cambridge". This latter canal later silted up, and by 1381, was no more.

Re-founded on or about the time the geomancer-king Offa of Mercia reconstructed the Great Bridge over the Granta, Cambridge has now no traces of this period, save the rapidly-dwindling street plan of the Borough (the Town north of the River).

About the millennium, Cambridge possessed a Minster, the monolithic cross of which was found in the last century

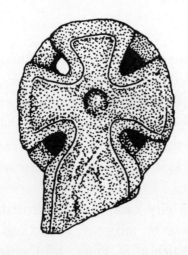

CROSS-HEAD FROM
CAMBRIDGE'S
SAXON MINSTER

under the rampart of the castle bailey. Cambridge had the largest fair in Europe, held on Sturbridge Common from antiquity until 1933. The Saxon King Edgar, among others, granted it a charter. Until the last century, the University claimed to have been founded by King Siegbert in 643 AD. As well as the undoubtedly Saxon St. Benet's, there is good evidence that the churches of St. Mary the Less, St. Botolph's, St. Edward's and St. Clement's are also pre-

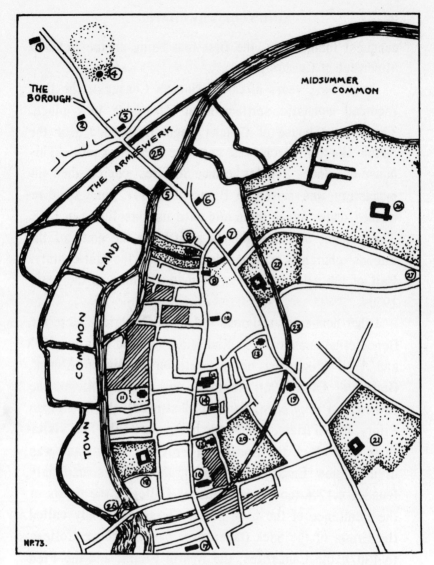

Cambridge at the time of the foundation of King's College. (The
Armeswerk was no longer extant but is shown for greater clarity).

1. All Saints' ad
   castra
2. St. Peter's
3. St. Giles' (canons
   regular)
4. Castle Hill
5. Great Bridge
   St. Clement's

7. St. Sepulchre's
8. Hospital of St John
9. All Saints' in the
   Jewry
10. St. Michael's
11. St. John Zachary
12. St. Mary's by the
    Market

13. Holy Trinity
14. St. Edward King
    and Martyr
15. St. Benedict's
16. St. Botolph's
17. St. Mary Minor
18. Carmelite Friary
19. St. Andrew's

20. Austin Friary
21. Dominican Priory
22. Franciscan Friary
23. King's Ditch
24. Benedictine nunnery
    of St. Radegund
25. The Armeswerk
26. The Mills
27. St. Radegund's Well

Monastic Land   **University & Colleges**

conquest foundations, the first four being on the 7-church alinement of Cambridge.

Twenty-six years after the Norman Conquest, the first recorded monastic settlement in Cambridge took place. This was a house of Canons Regular, founded near the Saxon Minster which was near the present castle. This house of Canons Regular became St. Giles' church when the monastery was moved to Barnwell in 1112, and there remained, under Augustinian rule until its dissolution in 1538. The present St. Giles' stands a little to the north of the Canons' church, which was demolished in the last century. Part of the site was taken for road-widening in the early 1960s.

Other houses of religious orders in Cambridge were the Benedictine nunnery of St. Radegund, founded between 1133 and 1138 (dissolved on the petition of Bishop Alcock, Bishop of Ely, 1496), which is now Jesus College; the Gilbertine Priory of St. Edmund (destroyed); the Dominican Priory, for 70 friars, Cambridge being one of the four visitations into which the Dominican Province in England was divided (now Emmanuel College); the Franciscan Friary, founded c.1226 (now Sidney Sussex College); the Friars of the Penitence of the Lord Jesus Christ, commonly called the Friars of the Sack (taken over by Peterhouse College in 1307); the Carmelites; the Austin Friars; and the Pied Friars.

As well as these Religious Orders, Cambridge was connected with the 'Fraternitas Sancti Sepulchri'—the Brotherhood of the Holy Sepulchre—a branch of the Knights Templar, who built the Holy Sepulchre church in Cambridge, as in London and Northampton. This was opposite the Hospital of St. John the Evangelist, a geomantic reconstruction of the situation of their namesakes in Jerusalem. This area was, in fact, the Jewry, as Cambridge had one of the largest Jewish populations in England. The Jews were expelled from England in 1290 on the order of King Edward I.

Two other Hospital foundations, the Hospital of St. Anthony and St. Eloy, and the leper Hospital of St. Mary Magdalene at Barnwell (the still-extant Stourbridge Chapel) complete the list.

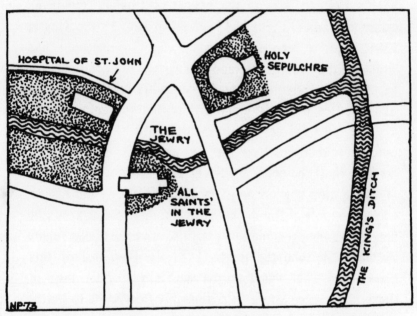

The Jewry at the time of the expulsion of the Jews from England.

From the above can be seen the continuing religious importance of Cambridge which led the founders and foundresses of the various colleges to endow their foundations. Cambridge in the middle ages was one of the major ports of England, having a flourishing trade with Continental ports on the North Sea coast. Sea-going vessels sailed up thru the Fen-lands along the rivers to Cambridge, and unloaded their wares at the numerous hithes which at that time lined the easterly bank of the Cambridge river. The common of Ships Green (now Sheep's Green) is a memory of the days when ship repairs were undertaken upon this piece of land. Sheep's Green is still a common, and a continuation of the world-famous 'backs', at the time of the construction of King's College, Town Commons.

The town of Cambridge, at the time of the foundation of King's College, was in the unique position of having no municipal rights. These had been taken away by the King in 1381, after a rebellion in which the Townspeople had wrecked the University and destroyed its charters and records. The University was subsequently given the powers and liberties normally granted to guilds and corporations, and the town did not regain control until 1856. Eight un-elected councillors from the University sat in each city council, until the boundary changes in 1973.

In the area now occupied by King's College and King's Lawn was part of the dockland, a thriving trading area with houses, warehouses and inns, and its own church, St. John's Zachary (St. John the Baptist). At the East end of this church was what was then the main street of the town of Cambridge, Milne Street. It ran roughly from South to North, parallel with High Street (now King's Parade), from a point near the Southern junction of the Saxon King's Ditch with the river. Where Milne Street reached the point where Trinity College Queen's Gate now stands, it turned East to join the High Street, the eastward extension being called St. Michael's Lane. Lanes ran off from Milne Street to serve the hithes on the riverside, linking the focal point of town, the market, with the transport facility. The market, serving both a port and the farming hinterland, had its own church, St. Mary by the Market, which had stalls and lean-tos built in the churchyard, which was really an extension to the market itself. This, too, was taken over by the University, and became Great St. Mary's, the so-called 'University Church'. It was rebuilt at about the same time as the construction of King's College Chapel.

The Saintly King Henry VI (who was later, in 1450, admitted to the craft of Freemasonry), founded, on April 2 (Passion Sunday) 1441, King's College of St. Nicholas of Bari, the patron saint of scholars, whose day, December 6th was also the King's birthday. King's College of St. Nicholas originally had provision for a Rector and twelve scholars, the typical number of a witches' coven, the occult master/disciples ratio. The land for the college was conveyed to the King in January 1440/1, and the foundation stone was laid by the King, in person, who was only nineteen years of age at the time. The buildings were of three full storeys and work proceeded slowly, finally being finished in a makeshift manner (which lasted for 380 years).

The original chapel, rarely mentioned in the guide books, stood between the South side of the Old Court (the original foundation) and the North side of the present chapel. It consisted of a chancel, nave and ante-chapel, having a door at the West end, and East and West windows. These were presumably of painted glass, as Henry VI brought from Flanders, in 1449, John Utnyam to make glass of all colours for Eton and King's Colleges. It was richly fitted up, and there are records of plate, hangings, relics, service books (illuminated manuscripts), vestments, choristers and both large and small organs. This original chapel was begun in 1441, and was consecrated by the Bishops of Salisbury and Lincoln in 1443. The original overseer of

Henry VI from the statue surmounting the lectern in the choir of King's College Chapel.

the works, John Langton, was consecrated Bishop of St. David's in the old chapel, on May 7th. 1447.

The original chapel fell down in 1537, having been in continuous use up to the eve of its collapse. A rise in the lawn on the north side of the present chapel marks the foundations of this original chapel. Services were transferred to the present chapel on the day the old one was wrecked, the final work on the present chapel being carried out on the orders of King Henry VIII after the fall of the old chapel.

The new chapel (the present one) was begun after Henry VI's decision to enlarge the college. This resulted in the renaming of the college as 'King's College of Our Lady and St. Nicholas in Cambridge', admitting only scholars from Eton College, King Henry VI's other foundation, King's College of the Blessed Virgin Mary of Eton beside Windsor. Qualified scholars at Eton were elected to scholarships, where they were taught logic and rhetoric, after three years of which they could proceed to a Fellowship to study theology, though law, medicine and astronomy were also studied. King's College claimed independence from the University, and, in 1453, an order was issued, forbidding scholars to take their degrees until they had formally renounced University jurisdiction. Fellows and scholars had their hair cut, compulsorily, and their beards trimmed by the porter, and sporting in any form was forbidden.

King Henry had decided upon a chapel of cathedral dimensions—35 feet longer than Oxford Cathedral—which naturally required an important omphalos—one which the previous chapel had adjoined. By August 1443, the King had begun to acquire the site. This lay between High Street and the river, extending from Clare College southward to the house of the Carmelite Friars in the area west of Milne Street, and from the south boundary of Henry's original site about the same distance southwards in the area between Milne Street and High Street. This area incorporated a large part of Milne Street itself, Piron Lane, which connected Milne Street to High Street, and two other lanes, Water Lane and Salthithe Lane, which led from Milne Street to the river. Included in this area was the church of St. John's Zachary and its vicarage, on the axis of which was to be built the new chapel. St. John's Zachary was demolished in 1444 in anticipation of the commencement of construction. God's House, a collegiate institution for grammar teachers, which had been recently established at the corner of Piron Lane and Milne Street, two taverns and a number of houses were acquired.

The salt hithe on the river was acquired from the Town, and a new way down to the river north of Trinity Hall was made by way of compensation. In 1447, the King took from the Town a large part of the commons on the other side of the river. These became the King's Backsides, now euphemistically shortened to 'the Backs'.

The foundation stone was laid by His Majesty at the site of the High Altar on St. James's Day, July 25th. 1446. This stone had an utmost occult importance, as it disappeared between the time of the foundation and the 18th. century, when William Cole, the Cambridge antiquary, wrote:

"About 1770, when they dug the Foundations of the new Altar, they searched very minutely for this stone, according to this direction (ie. the founder's will—NP); **but to no purpose. I was there with Mr. Essex the Architect more than**

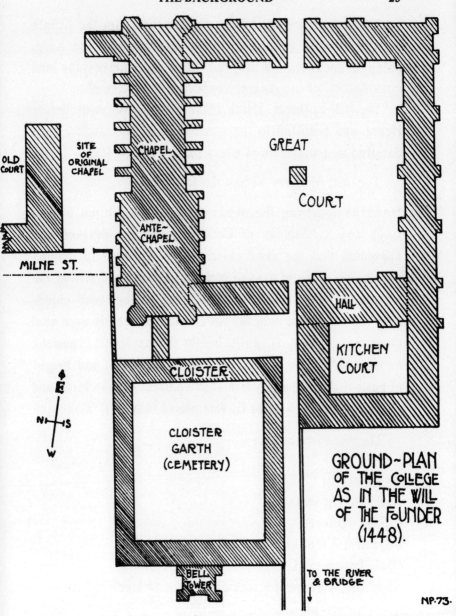

OLD COURT

SITE OF ORIGINAL CHAPEL

CHAPEL

GREAT

COURT

ANTE~CHAPEL

MILNE ST.

HALL

KITCHEN COURT

CLOISTER

E

N — S

W

CLOISTER GARTH (CEMETERY)

GROUND~PLAN OF THE COLLEGE AS IN THE WILL OF THE FOUNDER (1448).

BELL TOWER

TO THE RIVER & BRIDGE

NP.73.

once". The stone was placed at the omphalos, in the anticipation of the chapel's dimensions, as the part of land on
which the extreme easterly end of the chapel was to stand

was not purchased until 1451, three years after the King's Will. This will was not to imply the death of the King, being a document setting out the exact dimensions and construction of his college, especially the chapel.

The Will of Intent, March 12th. 1447/8, two years before Henry was admitted to the Craft of the Freemasons, gave detailed measurements of every part of the college.

The will of Henry VI has the following:

"And as touchyng the demensions of the Chirch of Our Lady and S. Nicholas of Cambridge, I have devised and appointed that the same chirche shal conteyne in lengthe cciiijxxviij fete of assyse without any yles and alle of the widenesse of xl fete and the lengthe of the same chirch from the west ende unto the Auters atte the queris dore shal conteyne cxx fete......walls height iiijxxx fete...... pament enhaunced iiij fete above the groundes without and height of pament of the quere j fete above pament of the chirch and pament at the high auter iij fete above that."

The measurements:
Length 288 feet
Width 40 feet
Walls Height 90 feet
Ceiling 80 feet
Pavement 4 feet above ground level
Choir Pavement 5 feet above ground level
High Altar Pavement 8 feet above ground level

The laying of the foundation stone marked the extension eastward of the axis of the dockland church of St. John's, in an analogous manner to the chancel extensions at Canterbury Cathedral, Westminster Abbey and countless other

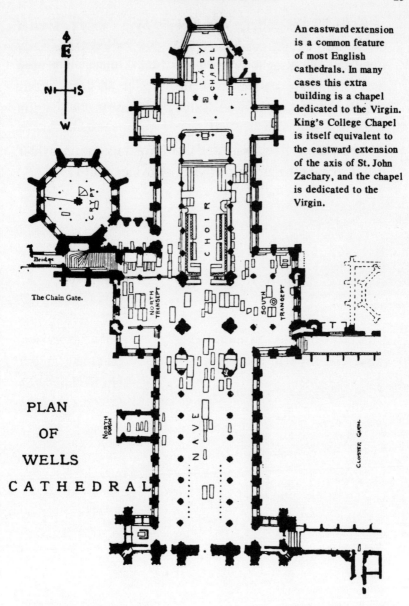

An eastward extension is a common feature of most English cathedrals. In many cases this extra building is a chapel dedicated to the Virgin. King's College Chapel is itself equivalent to the eastward extension of the axis of St. John Zachary, and the chapel is dedicated to the Virgin.

The Chain Gate.

PLAN

OF

WELLS

C A T H E D R A L

churches. On November 2nd 1446 (All Souls' Day), the cemetery of the new college, which was, in reality, the old churchyard of St. John's Zachary, was consecrated by the Bishop of Norwich.

Water for the college was brought by a conduit, similar to the still-extant conduit of 1327 now called the Trinity Conduit. The King's Conduit ran from a piece of ground near Madingley called Holwelle, a plot 30 feet square transferred by charter from Barnwell Priory to the King in 1444.

The chapel itself has walls of brick faced with ashlar, and incorporating a 'damp-course' of oyster shells.

2

The Work Begins

"To the honour of Almighty God, in whose hand are the hearts of Kings; of the most blessed and immaculate Virgin Mary, mother of Christ; and also of the glorious Confessor and Bishop Nicholas, Patron of my intended College, on whose festival we first saw the light."

The whole work of construction was to be committed to the supervision of William Wayneflete, Bishop of Winchester. The King also stipulated that the wages of the workmen should be as follows: £50 per annum (at that time a vast sum) for the master of works; £13 6s 8d for the clerk of works; £16 3s 4d for the chief mason; £12 8s 0d for the chief carpenter; £6 3s 4d for the chief smith.

There were three separate phases of construction, reflecting the turbulent times in which the chapel was erected. The initial period was from the foundation in 1446 until 1461, under the direction of the Master Mason Reginald Ely, when part of the eastern end was completed. When the question of authorship of the chapel is tackled, the credit has sometimes been attributed to the 'surveyor'. In the ground-plan and dimensional lay-out, King Henry VI himself is the author, under the canon of the Ancient Mysteries. Of the actual implementation, Reginald Ely 'Master Mason of

Our College Royal', appointed by a Patent of Henry VI **"to press masons, carpenters and other workers"** was the most important, being a master of his craft.

During this first period of construction, the general supervisors were as follows: (successively) John Langton, Chancellor of Cambridge University (altho King's claimed independence from that body, Langton was one of the original six members of King's and subsequently became Bishop of St. David's, being consecrated in the old chapel). For a short period in 1447, William Millington. Next was Nicholas Cloos, another of the original six, a Fleming, and sometime curate of St. John's Zachary. He retained the post of supervisor after his consecration as Bishop of Carlisle on March 14th 1449/50. Subsequently, Cloos was made Bishop of Lichfield (August 31st 1452). After Cloos' death in 1452, Robert Woodlarke, the Provost of King's, was appointed in December that year.

During this first period, up until 1461, when work ceased, Reginald Ely was master mason. After 1461, until his death in 1471, Ely was no longer connected with the construction of the chapel. In this pre-1461 period, the warden of the masons was John Brown. Thomas Sturgeon was master-carpenter, being named in impressment commissions both in 1443 and 1449. The name Sturgeon has a later connexion with the construction of the chapel, when, in 1480 John Sturgeon, possibly Thomas' son, and Martin Prentice received letters patent for the transport by water of timber for the chapel roof.

In 1449, Henry VI brought to England from Flanders a Flemish glazier, John Utnyam, to make glass for King's, but none ever reached the present chapel, so far as is known.

Before 1461, construction utilized stone from Thefdale (Jackdaw Crag or Petres Post) Quarry, 1½ miles south of Tadcaster in Yorkshire. This quarry was granted to the college in 1447. Stone was available from the Huddleston Quarry by 1446, and from King's Cliffe Quarry in Northamptonshire by June 1460. King's Cliffe was also the quarry from which the stone for Trinity College Great Gate and fountain was obtained. Before 1452, King's College had also acquired a clunch (chalk) quarry at Hinton (now Cherry Hinton, a suburb of Cambridge) Excepting that from this last quarry, all stone was carried by water to Cambridge.

After the capture of King Henry VI at the battle of St. Albans, worked slowed, altho Robert Woodlarke, Cloos' successor, writes:

Vaulting of Chapel completed before 1461 by ·Reginald Ely

(left)
This figure of a woodwose, wild man of the woods, also occurs as a former wooden roof-clave, now removed, in St. Alban's Cathedral. The iconography also represents the skull of Adam, from which grew a branch of the tree of knowledge, destined to become the true cross, upon which Christ was crucified.

(right)
Last Judgement, Gabriel's trump of doom.

(left)
Man with rope round neck. Allusion to Odin and halter used in masonic initiation.

(right)
Eagle roof-clave.

(left)
Ogma—sun face, similar to the deity on the tympanum of the Romano-British temple of Sul at Bath.

"When Henry VI was taken prisoner by the Earls of Salisbury and Warwick (battle of St. Albans, May 23rd 1455), **they pledged their word to him, in order to gain his good will, that they would hasten the completion of his church and all other building operations in Cambridge"**.

Work, in fact, continued, and the two north-easterly side chapels were completed at the time of the overthrow of the King. This was at the battle of Towton Moor, March 29th, 1461, in which 36,000 were killed. Subsequently, the King was murdered in prison, being buried hastily at Chertsey Abbey. The two side-chapels completed under the supervision of Reginald Ely are vaulted with lierne vaulting, so called because the ribs of the vault fancifully resemble 'lierre'—ivy. This lierne vaulting bears numerous claves (roof bosses), with markedly pagan connotations. One, illustrated here, bears a striking resemblance to the Ogma sun-face deity found at Bath, and another (also illustrated here) is a face with branches of oak bearing leaves emanating from the mouth, a woodwose, wild man of the woods, its oak leaves reminding one that the ancient Celtic builders of Gaul signed their work with an oak leaf. The ancient connexions of the oak with Druidism, the Celtic word **dru** meaning oak, are apparent.

Work lapsed in 1461, on the murder of the King, his captors having gone back on their word. It did not totally

Henry was born at Windsor in the year 1421. When Henry V was informed that Catherine had borne him an heir he asked: Where was the boy born? At Windsor was the reply. Turning to his Chamberlain, he gave voice to the following prophetic utterance:

" I Henry born at Monmouth,
 Shall small time reign, and much get;
 But Henry of Windsor shall long reign and loose all.
 But as God will, so be it."

cease, however, but continued in a desultory manner. On October 23rd 1467 the **"towers of the new church"** were covered in to protect the stonework from the ravages of frost. In 1472, the masons' lodge, first mentioned in a document of 1467, was rebuilt. The site of this is unknown. In 1476, receipt of donations **"pro fabrica nove ecclesia"** on behalf of the fabric of the new church—mark the re-

S.E. door label stop. Defaced by puritan iconoclasts. St. Margaret triumphant over the dragon.

commencement of work on a serious scale, as in 1477, £10 19s 4d was collected from the fellows of the college. In that year, John Bell, Warden of the Masons, was sent to Huntingdon to buy stone, Peterborough and Clipsham (Rutlandshire) stone also being purchased.

In 1479, Walter Field suc-ceeded Woodlarke. During Field's Provostship, between January 10th 1480/1, and June 14th 1483, receipts from the construction were £1240, and further stone was pur-chased, this time from Weldon, Hasilborough. Timber for roof-ing the completed portion was brought from Thaxted, Bardfield, Weybridge, Sapley, Canfield Park and Stansted Park. In the second phase of major work, in 1476, John Wolrych, who had been an ordinary Free Mason on Old Court in 1443, became Master Mason. Simon Clerk was his successor in 1477. Martin Prentice, first

known to be connected with the chapel in 1459, became
master-carpenter in 1480, and ceased to work on the project
before 1486. In 1480, the smiths working on the ironwork for
the second window on the south side were Simon Kendal
and Andrew Hacon.

Early in that year, parchment was bought on which to
make a plat (i.e. a scale drawing) of the roof **'in quo propo-
suit tractare tectum ecclesie'**, and oaks were purchased in
the same year from the Abbot of Walden. Clerk had previously been Master Mason at Walden church. The roof was

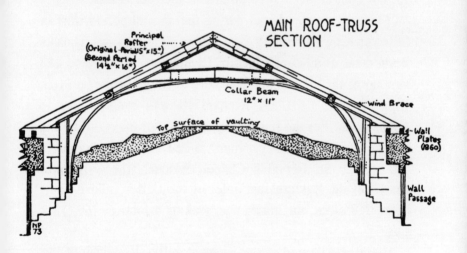

erected over the first five bays of the chapel by then
completed. Old-style arabic numerals can still be seen on
the roof trusses, numbered 1-6 (1480s) and 1-8 (later) and
moss was visible until the 18th century on the weathered
end which was left open to the riverside weather.

The roof is made with pairs of principals with wall-posts
cambered collar-beams and curved braces from wall-posts
to collars forming 4-centred arches (see section). Against
the piers, the posts and braces continue as far down as the

vaulting, but in the intermediate trusses, which are four feet wider, they stop irregularly, approximately two feet below the wall-plate. The rafters are laid flat and supported on two purlins on each side stiffened by two wind-braces. The work of Martin Prentice is distinguishable from the later carpentry by the double chamfering. All secondary timbers are chamfered. When the roof was leaded, firewood from the market was found to be too expensive, and wood was brought from Walden Park along with the roof-beams. According to H. Malden (1769), no spiders have ever appeared, nor cobweb been seen on any of the roof beams.

Funding for the chapel during the second period was as follows: King Edward IV contributed £1113 6s 8d; Thomas Rotherham, Bishop of Lincoln, Chancellor of England and another of the six original members of King's College, £100; King Richard III £750. Richard III was responsible, in August 1484, for the removal of the body of the mystic King Henry VI from Chertsey, where it had been ignominiously interred, to St. George's Chapel, Windsor, the Collegiate chapel of the Rosicrucian Order of the Garter, whose habit bears 168 stars, the garter one, making a total of 169 (13 x 13).

Miracles occurred at the geomantically-sited tomb of the King, to the south of the High Altar, but despite the tomb becoming an object of pilgrimage and veneration, two attempts at canonization of Henry VI have failed. The coffin of the King was opened, in the presence of members of King's College, in 1910, and a piece of silk was taken from the cloth in which the King's bones were wrapped, a relic preserved to this day at the college.

The master mason at this time, Simon Clerk of St. Edmundsbury, was also engaged on the construction of

Saffron Walden church, in Essex. Richard III, in reverence
to the late King Henry, sped the work, but his death at the
battle of Bosworth in 1485 stopped all work. It is interest-
ing to note that glass had been bought for the east window,
the north-east and south-east side windows. The south-east
window was only half a window, the lower half having a
planned building abutting onto it. William Neve, the King's
Glazier, and John Byrchold, the King's Serjeant Plumber
visited the chapel at the end of 1484 to supervize the
glazing of these windows.

At the defeat and death of Richard III, the chapel was
complete to the fifth bay westward, Roofed, but unvaulted,

Fan vaulting and panelling above great windows.

the brick walls above the ashlar facing inside, which were eventually intended to be covered up when the vaulting was erected, were painted white to reduce their conspicuousness. Without end towers, pinnacles or crenellations, the chapel's temporary entrance was by a door on the south side, in the fifth side-chapel westward, which was completed in June 1480.

Work had ceased in 1485, and Clerk died four years later. Work on the chapel did not resume in earnest after the demise of Richard III until 1508, when Henry VII, altho a notorious miser, had granted £1500 towards the completion of the edifice. Work resumed in full swing in March 1508/9, when John Wastell, the last great mediaeval-style master mason in England was appointed at a salary of £13 6s 8d per annum. The 'comptroller' at this time was William Swayne, succeeded in 1509 by John Lee. Harry Semerk was warden of the masons.

John Wastell, the master mason, had, between 1493 and 1505, designed and built the 'Bell Harry' tower at Canterbury Cathedral, the mother church of England, on the orders of Prior Goldstone. Wastell also constructed the eastern chapels at Peterborough Cathedral, the porch and pinnacles of Saffron Walden church (after 1485), the latter pinnacles being identical with those on King's College Chapel. He constructed the gatehouse of Trinity College (1491-2, 1496-7), and is believed to have been architect of the gateway of St. John's College, as typically Wastellian vaulting was used.

On March 24th 1508/9, Henry VII gave the college £5000, an astronomical sum for the time. The deed of conveyance stipulated that it was to be used entirely for building and finishing the chapel **"after like form and intent as it was**

ordered and devised by our uncle (Henry VI)'', without discontinuing or ceasing the work so far as the money would allow, and, if not completed during his lifetime, additional funds would be provided from his estate by his executors.

From 1509 to 1515, Richard Russell was master-carpenter. He constructed the last seven bays of the timber roof exactly to the pattern set by Prentice excepting the double chamfering. Russell's principals have a single stop-chamfer. Plumbers completed the roof-leading between April and December 1512.

Between October 1512 and August 1513, stone carvers. were employed in the chapel. Thomas Stockton, the King's Joiner was master-carver, from 1509 to 1515, and received an annual salary of £18 5s 0d. A joiner in charge of the stone carving explains the wood-carving technique used on the heraldic symbols in the ante-chapel. These heraldic devices were the first deviation from the hitherto purely sacred character of the chapel, as intended by the founder, to the secular pomp of the Tudors. In the first two periods, the carving in the chapel had no secular content except the Royal Arms of England, once. In the later period, heraldry ran rife, on both the interior and exterior walls. The heraldic beasts on the westerly buttresses originally had iron brackets on which to hang banners, which were flown on state occasions, as King's was, after all, a Royal foundation.

On February 8th 1511/12, another £5000 was granted to the college by the executors of the King's will, on condition that it was to be vaulted according to "**the form of a plat**". A plat was a technical drawing, either a plan or an elevation, and, in Tudor times, plats were used for communication

between the masons and the benefactors of the building. A series of plats sent from Boulogne by the master-mason engineer John Rogers, to Henry VIII in London is still preserved.

Double desks were made for the choir, and the windows were glazed, with figure-subjects, arms and badges as they should direct.

John Wastell commenced the vaulting, in Weldon Stone, in 1512, in the sum of £100 per severy (bay), the time stipulated being three years for completion. The fan vaults are in the form of rectangular portions of the four quadrants of an inverted concave conoid. According to Malden, the chapel clerk, 1759:

"...this roof is so geometrically contrived, that it would stand firm without either the walls or the key stone". (i.e. supported only by the buttresses and end towers-N.P.) **"The mystery of constructing vaults of this kind was the original secret of the Free-Masons: of whom John Wastell, the Master-Mason, contracted to employ not less than sixty, for carrying on the works of this chapel."**

The chapel having been intended by Reginald Ely to have the more pointed lierne vaulting, Wastell had to construct panelling above the windows in order to preserve the geo-mantic dimensions ordered by the founder-namely the ceiling height of eighty feet. Fan vaults were used more than a century earlier. The earliest surviving example is in the cloisters of Gloucester Cathedral 1370-1412. Sherborne Abbey, 1436-59 also had a major example.

The centres of the fan vaulting are composed of twelve large claves, or 'central keys'. These have, alternately, Tudor Roses and Portcullises carved by Thomas Stockton. They are 2'6" deep below the apex of the vault, and 3'5"

General view of one severy of Wastell's fan vaulting.

in diameter. On the top there is a **"square piece in the centre, where the lewis, or whatever other machine was used for the purpose of lowering the key into its place, is supposed to have been inserted"** (F. Mackenzie, 1841). Thus, at least, the last key was taken up into the roof and the vault completed, before the clave was finally lowered into place.

Having taken the completion of the vaulting in hand, Wastell was contracted in January 1512/13 to make twenty-one buttress finials

"accordyng to the fynyall of oon buttrasse which is wrought and sett up; except that all thies new fynyalles shal be made sumwhat larger in certain places acordyng to the mooldes for the same conceyvid and made".

This contract infers a kind of optical device, akin to that of entasis, which makes part of a building, or a whole building appear 'square' in perspective, as in the Parthenon at Athens. This is not done in modern office blocks, and so they appear to be falling over when one looks up at them. The northwest turret was completed at the same time as the finials. The optical device can no longer be checked, as the pinnacles were totally reconstructed in 1754, and further repaired in 1811 and 1875. They were patched up earlier this century, and a twelve-year scheme for replacing the parapets at the cost of £250000 was commenced in 1973. The end parapets were originally of a slightly different form, if the watercolour by J.M.W. Turner and the engraving by Harraden are accurate records of the chapel's west end at the time.

In March 1512/13, a third contract was made between the college and John Wastell for three more towers to match the first. Of the eastermost, the turret only was meant; for the westward, parts of the towers and the turrets.

These octagonal turrets are in six stages, with pilaster-like projections at the free corners, rising from pedestal bases superimposed on the main plinth, giving the effect of interpenetration of the plinth-mouldings thru the pedestal. The top of each turret, which is divided into two stages, rises free above the main parapet, the corner projexions

North-west label stop. Angel, defaced by puritans, carrying coat of arms of East Anglia, (or King Arthur).

continuing thru it as pinnacled standards. The faces of the octagon between the standards are filled with pierced stone latticework in the form of open quatrefoils in diagonal squares. These were described in Wastell's contract as 'cross-quarters'. The pinnacles of the standards and the crenellated parapets linking them form a corona round a crowning octagonal turret, which has a domical ogee crocketed cap of ashlar raised on a high drum pierced with quatrefoiled circles. Carved in high relief on the eight faces of the cap are alternate crowned portcullises and Tudor roses.

A fourth contract stipulated, in August 1513, the vaulting of 2 porches, 7 side-chapels, another 9 side-chapels "behind the quire", and all the crenellations of the porches and chapels. The vaults were to be finished by midsummer 1514 at a cost of £25 for the porches, and £20 and £12 each respectively for the elaborate and plainer vaults.

In 1515, the year Wastell is believed to have died, the chapel's stonework got as far as it ever would. The screen,

ϚEΠTRAL KEY TOP VIEW

which was to have been of stone, had abutments made, but was never erected. The original intention was to paint the interior, the normal Gothic practice at the time, blending the numerology, colour dimensions, incenses, music and ritual in a microcosmic expression of the splendour of God. This Gothic totality was a device to create a true cosmic consciousness, the product of a totally different ethos from that of a few years later, let alone the present day. The present puritanical interior is but a pale shadow of the masterful artistry which was envisaged by its architects. Each rib of the vault was to be coloured gules (scarlet), and the fan-background azure (blue). Gilded stars were to grace the blueness, and the ribs were to be outlined with gold. One chapel on the south side was started, and traces of paint can still be seen. The total scheme is visible today, in miniature, in the Chantry of Bishop Goldwell (died 1499) at Norwich Cathedral. The microcosm of the heavens with the pillars as trees, and the tracery-bars as branches with stars visible between them, inspired the early neo-gothic experiment of J. Hall, in 1798, which used ash-tree poles and willow branches. This experiment, however, was technical, and not spiritual, as examination of any 19th century neo-Gothic church will show.

Heraldic colours were to have graced the Royal coats of arms, and figures of saints were to have been erected in the tabernacles. The painting and embellishing was never implemented, due to lack of funds and to the end of Gothic architecture's recognized purpose. The alien choir-stalls and wooden screen attest to the total alteration in outlook during the Tudor regime, culminating in the dissolution of 645 monasteries, the suppression of 2374 chantries and free chapels, 110 hospitals, 90 colleges and the commencement of the siezure of the Common Lands from the common people of England.

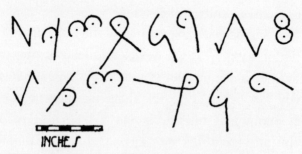

INCHES

Early Arabic numerals on roof trusses.

3

The Windows

On the completion of the stonework in 1515, the glazing commenced, as shown by a memorandum dated November 30th 1515, authorizing a payment of £100 by way of imprest to Barnard Floure, the King's Glazier, by Thomas Lark, the surveyor, the **"form and condition"** of the work being determined by Richard Foxe, Bishop of Winchester, one of Henry VII's executors. Floure was 'Almain' (German), and had been appointed Royal Glazier in 1505, much to the annoyance of the English Glaziers. He finished only the tracery glass and four of the great windows before his death, which was before 14th August 1517. From 1513 to 1516, Floure glazed the Savoy Hospital in London, using imported Rhenish glass.

After the death of Floure, nothing more was done until two contracts were placed (30th April and 3rd May 1526) to glaze the remaining twenty-two great windows; the glass put in during the reign of Richard III having been removed or destroyed.

Detail from the Harrowing of Hell, a demon issuing from the maw of the Beast. (From the Gospel of Nicodemus) Possibly influenced by Hieronymus Bosch, who died only 10 years before the window was designed, having himself designed stained-glass windows (executed by Willem Lombard and Henricken Bueken) for 'sHertogenbosch cathedral. (window 11, section 4)

Galyon Hone, a Dutchman, became Royal Glazier soon after the death of Floure, and was contracted to work on the chapel, which he did from 1526 to 1531. Subsequently, Hone worked on windows at Whitehall Palace, Hampton Court and Windsor Castle. He was assisted at Cambridge by two Londoners, Richard Bond and Thomas Reve, and another foreigner from the Flemish colony at Southwark (like Floure and Hone), James Nicholson. Nicholson glazed Great St. Mary's in Cambridge, which was then undergoing reconstruction, in 1518, but this glass is now all destroyed. He worked on the chapel from 1526 to 1528, then worked for Cardinal Wolsey at Oxford and elsewhere. About 1530, Nicholson gave up painting glass because of its supposed idolotrous nature, and became a printer, publishing three editions of the bible and New Testament, and several books of a heretical tendency.

Another Fleming from the Southwark colony was Francis Williamson, who worked in partnership with Symond Symondes, who had previously, in 1509, worked in Cambridge on the glazing of Christ's College. Christ's had been founded as the result of God's House being expelled from the site of King's in 1446, transferred by its founder William Bingham to St. Andrew's Street, granted a charter by Henry VII in 1505 for expansion under the aegis of Lady Margaret Beaufort. Symondes also glazed his own parish church, St. Margaret's, Westminster, which stands to the north of Westminster Abbey. All these glaziers had their workshops at either Southwark or London, most being Flemish of the Southwark School of glass-painting. The glaziers carried out the patterns of the designer, who, in most cases, was Dirick Vellert (1485-1544) of Antwerpen in Flanders. Vellert never came to England—his designs were sent across to the glaziers. The designs themselves bear a close resemblance to the windows, by Bernard von Orley, in St. Gudule's Cathedral in Brussels, and are mainly of the type and antitype theme–illustrations from the Old Testament or Apocrypha with their corresponding illustrations from the New Testament.

Travelling round the chapel, starting on the west end at the south side, the designer and glazier of each window were as follows:-

1/Unknown/Williamson and Symondes
2/Unknown/Unknown
3-7/Vellert/Hone
8-11/Vellert/Reve
12/Vellert/Reve (lower half, originally upper half)
    Hedgeland (upper, 1845)
13/Vellert/Hone
14/Vellert/Bond
15/Vellert/Reve
16/Vellert/Hone (upper) Unknown (lower)
17/Vellert/Hone, Coeke/Reve, Unknown
18/Vellert/Reve
19/Unknown/Nicholson
20/Vellert/Reve
21/Unknown/Nicholson
22 Vellert/Hone
23/Unknown/Williamson and Symondes
24/Floure designer and glazier
25/Unknown/Williamson and Symondes

The twelfth window in the chapel was meant to have a building, part of Great Court (see diagram, page 23), abutting onto it. The partially-built construction was torn down in 1827 when William Wilkins' neo-gothic plan for completing the court was under way. This fragment of building was all that was finished of the founder's original court, and the window was rebuilt to conform with the others. It was glazed by Hedgeland, of whom more later.

The finance for the window-glass came from a Praemunire (church fine) incurred by the onetime Bishop of Norwich, Richard Nix (died 1536). Nix, who had gone blind, having been what is described as a 'persecutor', was fined the enormous sum of £10000 for illegally extending his jurisdiction over the Mayor of Thetford.

The layout of the windows is identical to the mnemonic diagram in Robert Fludd's (1574–1637) **'Technical History of the Microcosm'**, in the section **'Ars Memoria'**. At King's College, the layout is as follows:-

The central panel bears the four 'messengers', figures bearing scrolls upon which are painted quotations from relevent passages in the Bible and Apocrypha There are 94 messengers in all drawn from only 42 originals. The great East window does not have 'messengers', and the messengers' panels are omitted from the following list.

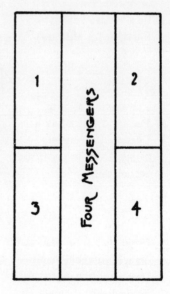

The subjects of the windows, the finest intact series in England, are as follows:-

1

1. The translation of Enoch
2. Solomon receives his Mother, Bath-Sheba
3. Assumption of the Virgin
4. Coronation of the Virgin

2

1. The death of Tobit
2. The burial of Jacob
3. The death of the Virgin
4. The burial of the Virgin

3

1. Paul exorcizing the woman with the spirit of divination
2. Paul before the Chief Captain Lysias at Jerusalem
3. Paul's farewell at Philippi (or Miletus)
4. Paul before the tyrant Nero

4

1. Conversion of Saul
2. Paul conversing with disciples at Damascus
3. Paul and Barnabas at Lystra. The priest brings oxen to sacrifice before them
4. Paul stoned at Lystra

5

1. Peter and John heal the cripple at the Temple
2. The arrest of the Apostles
3. Peter and the Apostels going to the Temple. In the background, Peter inside, preaching
4. Death of Ananias

6

1. Elijah transported heavenward in a chariot of fire
3. The ascension of Christ

2. Moses receiving the Tables of the Law from God's Hand on Mount Sinai
4. The descent of the Holy Spirit

7

1. Return of the prodigal son
3. The unbelief of the doubting Thomas

2. The meeting of Jacob and Joseph in Egypt
4. Christ appearing to the Apostles less Thomas

8

1. The angel Raphael, disguised as a young man, meets Tobias
3. Christ, disguised as a traveller, meets the two disciples going to Emmaus

2. Habakuk feeding Daniel in the lions' den
4. The supper at Emmaus, Christ recognized by the breaking of the bread

9

1. Reuben at the pit finds Joseph gone
3. The three Marys at the Sepulchre, finding it empty

2. Darius visits the lions' den, and finds Daniel alive
4. Christ, with a spade, appears to Mary Magdalene in the garden

10

1. Jonah vomited up by the Whale
3. The resurrexion of Christ

2. Anna, the mother of Tobias, who had given him up for dead, sees him return with Azarius
4. Christ appearing to his mother at prayer

Elijah is translated to Heaven in the fiery aerial chariot, casting his mantle down to Elisha standing below. (window 6, section 1)

Darius visits the lions' den, and finds Daniel alive. (window 9, section 2)

11

1. Joseph cast into the pit
   by his brothers
3. The burial of Christ

2. Israel going out of
   Egypt. Pharoah's host
   drown in the Red Sea
4. Christ overcoming the
   Devil and Hell

12

Upper half not part of schema; 19th century

3. Naomi and her
   daughters-in-law
   lament her husband
   Elimelech

4. The Virgin and other
   Holy women lamenting
   over the dead Christ

13

Tracery: In the centre, the arms of Henry VII on a banner held by
a red dragon; in the side-lights, the red rose of Lancaster, and
the red-and-white Tudor Rose, the feather of truth with the scroll
Ich Dien, the fleur-de-lys and the initials HR, HE and HK. Ich
Dien, one of the two mottoes of the Black Prince, has been
applied to the Princes of Wales ever since. It is believed (according to A.P. Stanley, 'Memorials of Canterbury', 1868) that "the
Welsh Antiquaries maintain that it is a Celtic and not a German
motto "Behold the Man", the words used by Edward I on present-
ing his first-born son to the Welsh". In this window, the mnemonic layout is not used. There are no messengers with inscriptions,
and in the first three lights below the transom is the Ecce Homo
(behold the Man). In the centre three, Pontius Pilate is washing
his hands. In the centre, Christ is represented with His back to
the spectator. In the three on the right, Christ is shown, bearing
the cross, with Saint Veronica offering her napkin to Our Lord to
wipe His face, whereupon it took on the image of His face, and
now is one of the four great Relics preserved in the piers of the
dome at St. Peter's at Rome.
Above the transom, the left three lights contain the nailing to
cross. In the centre, Christ is shown crucified between the two
thieves. In the right three lights, Christ's body is taken down
from the cross.

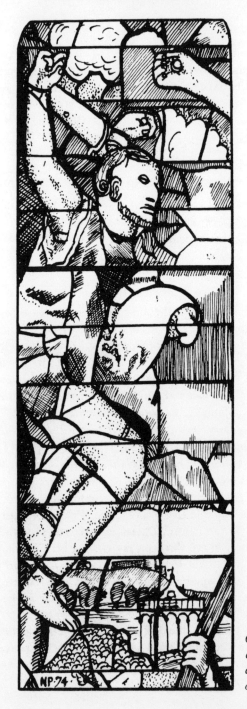

One of the malefa
crucified with C
according to the g
of St. Luke (windo

14

1. The torment of Job by three demons
2. Crowning of Solomon
3. The scourging of Christ
4. Christ crowned with thorns

15

1. Jeremiah in prison
2. Noah mocked by Ham
3. Christ before Annas
4. Christ before Herod

16

1. Cain kills Abel
2. Shemei curses King David
3. The Kiss of Judas. Peter attacks Malchus, who has on his left arm NALCKEN
4. Christ blindfolded and mocked

17

1. The fall of manna
2. The fall of the rebel angels
3. The last supper
4. Christ's agony in the garden. The Holy Grail is shown at the left upper corner

18

1. Elisha raises the Shunammite's son
2. The triumph of David
3. The raising of Lazarus
4. The entry of Christ into Jerusalem

19

1. Naaman the leper washing himself in the Jordan
2. Jacob tempts Esau to sell his birthright
3. Christ's baptism
4. The temptation of Christ

20

1. The Golden Calf, on a pillar of ruby, being worshipped by the Jews. Moses casts down the Tables of the Law. On them is the Flemish *"DUS ELSTE LIEF GODT BOVE ALEN"* (Thou shalt love God above all)

2. The massacre of the Seed Royal by Athaliah

3. The idols of Egypt are cast down. At the bottom is the number 15017, read by some as a date (1517)

4. The massacre of the innocents

21

1. The purification of women under the law

3. The presentation of Christ in the Temple

2. Jacob's flight from Esau

4. The flight into Egypt

22

1. The circumcision of Isaac by Abraham

3. The circumcision of Christ

2. The visit of the Queen of Sheba by Solomon

4. The adoration of the Magi

23

1. The temptation of Eve

3. The annunciation

2. Moses and the burning bush

4. The nativity

24

1. The Presentation of the golden table in the Temple of the Sun. Valerius Maximus tells the story as follows *"Someone had purchased the produce of their next cast from some fishermen who were drawing their nets near Miletus. They brought up a*

great golden Delphic Table (or tripod) and a dispute arose; they
said they had sold their catch of fish, the other asserted that he
had bought whatever the cast might bring up. It was agreed to
consult the oracle of Apollo at Delphi, who said: "He who is
the first of all men in wisdom, to him let the tripod be given."
So they offered it to Thales of Miletus. He, in modesty yielded it
to Bias of Prione, and he to Pittacus: thus it went the round of
the Seven Wise Men of Greece, till it reached Solon of Athens
who, judging the god to be the wisest, offered the prize to
Apollo". This is taken to be the type of 3. the presentation of
the Virgin in the Temple.

2. The Marriage of Tobias and Sara
4. The Marriage of Joseph and Mary

25

1. Offering of Joachim and Anna rejected by the High Priest
3. Joachim and Anna at the Golden Gate of the Temple

2. Joachim is bidden by an angel to Jerusalem, where he would meet his wife at the Golden Gate of the Temple
4. Anna gives birth to the Virgin Mary

Subsequent to their completion, the windows were repaired in 1570-71, 1591-92, 1616-17, re-leaded and had saddle-bars renewed 1657-59, repaired 1711-12, 1720-21 and 1725-30, where Belcher was paid £523 for the work.

In 1757-65, at the cost of £1600, the stonework of the reveals and mullions was renewed, and the windows were patched and re-leaded. Between 1842 and 1849, J.P.Hedgeland, at a cost of £200 per window, patched and re-leaded and 'restored' a large part of the glass. This involved at least one 'new' head on a figure, and the obliteration of scrolls etc. In **The Guardian** No. 7, November 21st 1849, a protest over 'this work of destruction' finally succeeded in stopping Hedgeland's vandalism. Between 1893 and 1906, the windows untouched by Hedgeland's heavy hand were restored by C.E. Kempe. During the Second World War, all the glass—except the tracery was removed to an underground bunker, and was cleaned, re-leaded and photographed before it was replaced—as late as 1951.

4

The Fittings

On completion of the painted glass (excepting the west end), the interior fittings were due to be installed. At this point, the original Perpendicular Gothic was abandoned, and a wooden screen in the so-called 'renaissance' style was made by foreign craftsmen, probably Italian, between June 1533 and May 1536. It is as wide as, and in the same position as that stipulated by the founder. The west window was glazed plain, as money had run out on Fisher's imprisonment for opposing Henry VIII's divorce (October 1530). It was glazed by the company of Clayton and Bell in 1878-79. The money for the screen etc was provided by Henry VIII after a petition from the college to complete the high altar and sixteen others, of stone; the entire paving; the screen; the metal fittings; stalls; doors; images and painting and gilding the main vault. The cost was estimated at £2893.

At this period in England's affairs, Protestant tracts

had been arriving in Cambridge from North Germany, and a sect of protestants known as the Germans met at the White Horse Inn in the town. In 1535, the Guild of Corpus Christi was suspended, later restored by Mary, it was finally suppressed by Elizabeth 1. The canopy covering the Host took fire during the last procession of the Guild, and was held to be an omen. In 1538, the dissolution of the monasteries began, and, in 1545, an Act for the dissolution of the Universities was drawn up. However, it was not put into effect. King's, with a revenue of £1010, appealed to Katharine Parr to intercede with the King, which she did successfully.

The chapel was just about finished, when the religion for which it was built was destroyed. Its opening, when the old chapel collapsed, was at the time of the dissolution. The purpose had changed, but the building remained, its innate numerology testimony to its true purpose—an instrument of enlightenment, an enlightenment destroyed in Protestant countries by the Reformation itself, and in the Catholic ones by the pernicious acts of the Society of Jesus—the Jesuits.

The subsequent history of the chapel is of constant alteration and change. An organ was not installed until 1606, (by Dallam), and was taken down, and the pipes sold, by order of Parliament during the Commonwealth. The windows survived the puritanical zeal of William Dowsing, the Civil War church wrecker, possibly thru the appointment of Dr. Whichcote as Provost of King's College by the Long Parliament. Legend has it that Dowsing accepted a bribe of 6s 8d from the Dean to spare the windows. This is unlikely, as a religious mania, not personal aggrandisement, was the drive of the maniac Dowsing. Another, equally implausible, legend, is that all the windows were taken out, some say in one night by a man and a boy, and buried before Dowsing's hammer descended on the chapel. In fact, only a few carvings suffered the hammer blow of iconoclasm.

The present organ was built in 1688 by Rene Harris, but has suffered at least three reconstructions since then. The

NP.73.

Side chapel window from the outside showing two types of tracery.

north, south and west doors were made in 1614-15 by Henry Man. At the same time, the trees, cherubim and tetragrammaton were carved in the tympanum at the west end.

The stalls date from between 1536 and 1538. The cost of both stalls and screen was £1333 6s 8d.

King's College Chapel proper has eighteen side-chapels, some of which were once used as chantries. Chantries were until their suppression during the Reformation, private chapels, each endowed by an individual in order that masses might be sung until the Last Judgement for the health of the soul of the departed. In King's College Chapel, each side-chapel is 20 feet 6 inches by 12 feet, a dimension produced by inscribing Solomon's Seal in a circle (see diagram.) The eighteen side-chapels lie in the spaces formed between ten of the eleven buttresses on the northern and southern side of the chapel proper. They have the main plinth of the chapel continued across their external faces, horizontal cornices carved with portcullises, Tudor roses, fleur-de-lys and foliated paterae, and pierced parapet walls. These pierced parapet walls are continued at a higher level over the north and south doors. The side-chapel walls are composed mainly of broad eight-light windows. On each side of

Vaulting of side chapel completed by John Wastell 1513-15

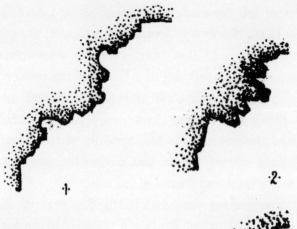

Plan of mouldings of vaulting
shafts in the side-chapels:
(1) Pre 1461·
(2) Post 1461 original type
(3) Post 1461 simplified after
*   completion*

the chapel proper, the upper portions of the windows have, in all, thirteen curvilinear panels and five rectilinear.

Henry VI's original scheme intended fewer side chapels. The departure from the Will of the Founder is that it envisaged only those connected to the ante-chapel, and a two-storey vestry 50 by 22 feet, divided into two rooms on each floor north of the choir (ie. the side of Old Court, and next to the old chapel). This is one of the few departures from the original plan, providing what later became chantries of King's College officials.

On the South side, the second chapel from the west was the chantry of Robert Hacomblen, D.D.. Hacomblen was provost when some of the great windows were erected, wrote **'Comments on Aristotle's Ethicks'**, and donated the brass lectern which now stands in the choir. In the glass of this chapel are the evangelistic symbols and the four fathers of the Latin church—St. Jerome, St. Ambrose, St. Augustine and St. Gregory. In this chantry is the monumental brass of Hacomblen, consisting of a figure of Hacomblen in surplice and almuce with a scroll from the mouth with an inscription in gothic black-letter characters upon it, a marginal inscription-fillet bearing the four symbols of the evangelists, one at each corner, and a shield showing the five wounds of Christ, retaining traces of red enamel.

The chapel immediately to the east of Hacomblen's Chantry is Provost Brassie's Chapel, where he was buried in 1558(Provost 1556-8). Robert Brassie, S.T.P., is depicted on his memorial brass dressed in surplice, almuce and stole. The brass shows traces of an inlay of white metal. Below the figure is a plate with a gothic inscription in Latin which, translated, reads **"Here lies Robert Brassie, Doctor of Divinity, formerly Provost of this College, who departed this life November 10, A.D. 1558"**. Two shields, and a scroll from the mouth have been destroyed by iconoclasts.

The easternmost chantry on the south side was the chantry of John Argentine provost from 1501-1507. In this chapel is another monumental brass. This shows the figure of a man in academic dress, with an inscription on a scroll from his mouth. Below the effigy is an inscription-plate. On the scroll is a Latin supplication, which, translated, reads **"O Christ, Son of the Virgin, Crucified Lord, Redeemer of Mankind, remember me"**. On the inscription plate are the words (again in Latin) **"This stone buries the body of John Argentine, Master of Arts, Physician, Preacher of the Gospel; Passenger, remember, thou art mortal, pray in an humble posture, that my soul may live in Christ, in a state of immortality"**. On a fillet around the stone upon which

Internal frontage of side-chapel on north side of ante-chapel showing arms of Henry VII. Tracery of 26 elements.

brasses are mounted is written (in Latin) **"Pray for the soul of John Argentine, Master of Arts, Doctor of Physick and Divinity, and Provost of this college, who died February 2, 1507, May God have mercy on his soul. Amen"**. In the corners of the fillet were the four evangelists' symbols, those of St. Mark and St. Matthew now being missing, the other two retaining traces of red enamel. There were also four shields, three of which are still extant with the arms of Argentine. A scroll and crucifixion have been destroyed by puritan fanatics. In 1920-21, this chantry was converted into a war memorial chapel to commemorate the 1914-18 World War, and re-named the All Souls Chapel.

On the north side of the chapel is the chantry of William Towne. This contains the oldest monumental brass in King's College Chapel, and was the first part to be roofed, before 1461. Towne's chantry, the second from the east, commemorates William Towne, DD., who was a Fellow of King's. The brass shows an effigy of a man in academic dress holding a scroll (defaced) in Gothic writing. Below is a plate with a Latin inscription (the supplication partially defaced by puritan vandalism) **"Pray for the soul of master William Towne, Doctor of Divinity, once a Fellow of this College, who died on the eleventh day of March 1494. Whose soul God Pardon. Amen."**

The side-chapel second from the west on the north side was fitted out as a memorial to the founder, in 1930-32.

The windows of the side-chapels are filled with a multiplicity of fragments of glass, mostly of mediaeval date. In the first chapel from the east on the northern side, there are, inter alia, fragments dug up when the Old Cavendish Laboratories were built, originally in the Augustinian Priory. Remnants of the original glass in the first three

*Interior
of ante-chapel
looking Westward
towards the disused
West Door. This ante-chapel
has the same proportions in a
foot-for-cubit ratio as the Temple of
Solomon formerly at Jerusalem.*

chapels from the east on the north side show that originally
there were at least ten apostles and eight prophets represented. In the second chapel from the east are panels which
were originally in the old East range of the Schools,
removed in 1748, and obtained by an exchange of glass with
the church at Greenford, Middlesex. The fourth chapel from
the east on this side has the scratchings 'Thos. Stevens
Glazier. 1761.' and 'James Mills, Glazier and Plumber,
cleaned these windows.....John Leach Feb. 1806'. In the
next side-chapel westward is the scratching 'John Hennebert
Plumber and Glazier, 1767'. In the second from westernmost
on the north side, amongst many other pieces are two
quarries with windmills, inscribed 'As God will 1557'. The
window of the westernmost side chapel on the north is composed in the main of glass dating from 1850, other than the
coat of arms of Benjamin Whichcote, Provost 1644-60,
signed and dated John Clarke, 1650. This, however, was
inserted in 1924.

On the southern side, the easternmost chantry, that of
Argentine, the windows contain an early 16th century Flemish or Rhenish glass, which was, however, put in in 1920.
Another part of the window has a figure of God the Father,
originally from La Chenu church, north of Tours in France.
Flemish glass can be found in the next chapel, but again,
altho authentic, was bought from St. Catharine's college in
1921. In the third chapel from the west on the south side
there is much original glass, heavily restored in 1857 by
Constable. One quarry is inscribed with the name of Robert
Brassie. In the next chapel west, the majority of glass is by
Constable, 1857, excepting the four founders of the Latin
Church, which date from around 1520. The scratching 'John
Barker 1744 Glazier and Plumber' can also be detected. The

last side-chapel has glass which bears the arms of Martin Freeman, Fellow of King's, died 1630, of the same date.

The fragmentary nature of the side-chapel windows, with consequent lack of original glass, is a reminder of an iconoclastic past and savage 'restorations'—as the artistic vandalism of the eighteenth, nineteenth and twentieth centuries is known. Between 1920 and 1930, the amount of painted glass was increased from twenty lights in five chapels to fifty-seven in nine chapels, excluding the tracery lights, much of which is original.

The side-chapels are, in general, floored with square red tiles, tho there are two examples of mid-14th century incised tiles, possibly from St. John's Zachary. Two others are of smashed stone slabs. The side-chapels are roofed with lead. On the fourth chapel from the west on the north side, on the roof was an inscription cast in lead sheeting, recording the re-leading of **'these small chapels'** in 1829 by T. Greef, Plumber.

In 1633, Thomas Weaver gave the panelling with armorial bearings. The canopies were made between 1675 and 1678 by Cornelius Austin at the cost of £305. In 1678-79 Austin added the panelling over the north and south doors further east. This panelling was torn out in the mid-1960's under the plan of Robert Maguire and Keith Murray, carried out by Sir Martyn Beckett, Bart. This act of destruction revealed a considerable amount of medieaval inscriptions, one of a horse, another the date April 29th 1524, and others, semilegible. The oak pulpit, hexagonal, with four linenfold panels in each face in moulded panelling, open below and with corner styles continued to form legs, is now in the church of St. Edward, King and Martyr.

The arrangements and fittings of the east end have been

West End. Tudor Rose with figure now said to be Elizabeth of York c. 1510. Malden (1769) however wrote: "In the middle of these Roses (on the West Side, towards the South) may be seen a small figure of the Virgin Mary: After which foreigners make frequent enquiries, and never fail to pay it a religious reverence; crossing their breasts at the sight, and addressing it with a short prayer."

changed and modified on numerous occasions, for both religious and 'aesthetic' reasons. In the reign of Queen Elizabeth I, who attended two services and a performance of the play **'Aulularia'** by Plautus in the chapel on the same Sunday, the high altar was ripped out and destroyed. This was in the alleged 'renaissance' style. The fate of the other sixteen altars planned is not known. They were rendered obsolete by the alteration in litany upon the foundation of the Church of England, of which Cambridge was, and is, a major centre.

In 1633 and 1634, Woodroffe built a screen across the east end, forming a reredos, the communion table being set against it and railed about. An entirely new arrangement was designed by James Essex, with stonework by Jeffs and Bentley and woodwork by Cotton and Humfrey, was begun in 1770, and finished in 1776 at the cost of £1652. James Essex was the architect of the old Guildhall of Cambridge, 1782.

Thomas Garner made a new altar in 1902, and a new reredos, communion rails and panelling were made by Detmar Blow and Ferdinand Billery (1911). All this survived but half a century, as, in 1960, Robert Maguire and Keith Murray were appointed to **"re-establish the high altar visually and liturgically as the focal point** (sic) **of the chapel".** These two had already decided to tear out the panelling back to the choir stalls, when, in May 1961, Major A.E. Allnatt donated a £275000 Rubens painting **'The Adoration of the Magi'.** In its original site, the Carmelite Convent at Leuven in Flanders, the painting had been the high altarpiece.

Ornament on wall below west window,
by Thomas Stockton c. 1508

Allnatt stipulated that it must be set on the east-west axis. Maguire and Murray originally intended to use the altar as the sacrificial centrepiece, bringing it a bay and a half nearer the congregation, with the priest celebrating Holy communion in the westward-facing position, in the mistaken 'liturgical renewal', an admission of the inevitable failure to reconcile agnostic Christianity with centuries-old symbolic ritual. The introduction of the compulsory Rubens' Adoration forced the architects to carry the destruction of the sanctuary to an even greater degree. The plan was evolved to demolish the altar platform, despite the fact that this was an essential part of the founder's plan.

Maguire was removed, as he was considered obstructive by the College, and Sir Martyn Beckett, Bart., an aristocratic architect who had worked for the National Trust on Stately Homes, was appointed. His scheme was completed in 1968. The result is a botch-up job, attempting to mix perpendicular and renaissance with 1960s coffee-bar modern without regard to the true purpose of the chapel as a microcosm of creation. £110000 was spent on this travesty, which, at least, fits in with King's TV image, the sacred showbiz of Christmas Eve and the record and literature stall, the tables of the money-changers, the chapel ringing with the litany of the till.

5

The Rest of the Developments

Fuller, in his church history, writes "**The whole college was intended conformable to the chapel: but the untimely death (or rather deposing) of King HENRY the Sixth hindred the same**". Stow, in his chronicle, says "**I suppose that if the rest of the House had proceeded according to the chapel already finished as his** (Henry VI - NP) **full intent and meaning was, the like College could scarce have been found again in any christian land.**" Loggan's print of 1688 shows a lightning conductor on the finial of each ogee crocketed cap. The invention of lightning conductors is generally ascribed to Benjamin Franklin, who lived a century later.

For many years, the only College buildings were the chapel and Old Court. Brick Building, south-east of the chapel, was built in the seventeenth century, being finished in 1693. It lasted until the nineteenth century. The separate bell tower, of wood, fell into disrepair, and was removed in the eighteenth century. The site of the bell tower, thirty

yards from the west door, can be seen as 'crop-patterns' in
aerial photographs. Early views of the college show a pair
of bowling greens next to the river, the space between them
and the chapel being exactly the size of the cloister direct-
ed by the founder, but never built. These disappeared at
the laying out of King's Lawn in 1772.

Subsequent to Brick Building's completion, nothing was
done to further the completion of the founder's scheme until
Dr John Adams, Provost from 1712-20 started a building
fund. In 1714, Toft Monk's wood, which belonged to the
College, was cut down and the wood sold for £2640, which
was put in the fund. In 1713, Nicholas Hawksmoor, aided
by Sir Christopher Wren, prepared plans and scale models
for the completion of the college. In the neoclassical style,
they contained a cloister and bell tower in the same place
as decided upon by Henry VI. This was to have been part
of the grand scheme for Cambridge, the last plan which
perpetuated the old market-river link. Money was not
forthcoming.

In 1724, James Gibbs was paid to draw up plans for a
court 240 feet by 282 feet. In 1724, the foundation stone to
the only part built, the Fellows' Building, was laid. It was
built by Christopher Cass, citizen and mason of London,
and Gibbs was not paid finally until 1759. The foundation
stone of Gibbs' Building was the block with a saw-cut
across it which stands in the foreground of Loggan's 1688
engraving. It was being sawn by two freemasons when news
of the death of Henry VI arrived. Packing up their tools,
they left, thinking that the building would never be completed. The stone then stood in the green beside the chapel
from 1461 until 1724, when it was used as the foundation
stone.

The chapel as seen across the roofs behind King's Parade.

In 1784, Robert Adam drew up a scheme for completion, but to no avail, the same fate as the neo-gothic plans of 1795 by James Wyatt. William Wilkins, in 1823, produced a plan, which was submitted to a committee of Wilkins himself, Jeffry Wyatt and John Nash, after having won first prize in a competition for the completion. It included a plan to gothicize the neoclassical Gibbs Building. Other buildings were demolished, and the scheme was built between 1824–1828. The first dinner was held in the newly-completed hall on February 27th 1828. The screen wall which to-day fronts on King's Parade replaced houses, the buildings in front of the college had been demolished, and railings were erected. The screen was intended to be one wall of a covered walk, never built. The railings were sawn off in the second world war, at the same time St. John's College was erecting new ones—the date 1940 can be seen on the railings and gateway opposite the Holy Sepulchre church.

The bridge dates from 1819, and is the work of Wilkins. It cost £3771, and replaced the bridge, further downstream, on the founder's site, which had been rebuilt from the original (1472-73) in 1627 by George Thompson, and condemned by Rennie in 1818.

The fountain in the centre of Great Court was designed by H.A. Armstead, and built in 1879.

Thus, from being a building amongst buildings, the Chapel became the focal point of Cambridge University, whilst not being afforded the honour of becoming the University church. During the latter part of the seventeenth century, subsequent to the puritan mania, and the Newtonian enlightenment (Newton was nominated Provost of King's, by King William III but the College would not permit it, allegedly on the technicality that Newton was a layman), the colleges declined in fortune, and the University nearly went out of being for the second time. But the University closed the river towpaths, and the fens were drained. Commerce, being thwarted, had a canal surveyed in 1778, to link Cambridge to London. This was never started. The railway was kept at a 'safe distance' from King's College Chapel, three miles away in the enclosed Middle Field.

King's Parade, from being High Street, became a piece of 'townscape', almost a stage set. Surrounded by masterpieces—all fake relics of former ages. The Senate House, designed by Gibbs and built between 1722 and 1768, was part of a larger scheme, unbuilt thru lack of funds. It is in

Cory's Buildings, the White Horse and Black Bull Inns, contemporary with the chapel, all demolished with the exception of the Black Bull—now part of King's College. The last demolition was in 1930 for the frontage of St. Catharine's College.

Design for the Bell Tower
(see plan, page 23)

(from an engraving in Lyson's 'Britannia' after an original drawing in the British Museum)

The will of intent of Henry VI included a Cloister, the west end of which was to contain a Tower 24 feet square (the size of one severy in the Chapel), 120 feet in height to the corbel table, above which were to be four turrets terminating in pinnacles. The original drawing (a plat) measures 52 x 15 inches and is lettered "Campanile Collegii Regalis Cantebrigiae". It is of late 15th century/early 16th century design, similar in proportion to John Wastell's Bell Harry Tower at Canterbury Cathedral The external panelling resembles the work of William Vertue and Robert Vertue (designers of Bath Abbey) at the Henry VII Chapel in Westminster Abbey. A wooden belfry was erected 150 feet to the west of the chapel when lack of money prevented the completion of the founder's scheme. This was demolished in 1739.

Chichester cathedral has the only surviving detached bell tower in England.

The Northwest corner of Old Court, as in the year 1815. Milne Street deviated to the right at this point, and the original college entrance still exists, much 'restored' just round the corner. All but the lower part of this gateway, saved by public outcry when partially destroyed, was demolished in 1835. The present buildings were designed by G.G. Scott, 1864 and J.L. Pearson, 1890.

the Corinthian style, and, behind its 1789-92 cast-iron railings stands another part of the stage set for which King's College Chapel is so famous–the fake Warwick Vase. This copy, given by Hugh, third Duke of Northumberland to Cambridge University in 1842, was made in about 1830 by Sir Edward Thomason at Birmingham. It stands on a cast-iron block, which, until 1936 had a wooden casing, painted to resemble stone. It is now encased in real stone, with lettering by Eric Gill. Opposite the Senate House, forming the end of King's Parade, is the fake chateau of Gonville and Caius College. This replaced houses in the last century, and there are photographs extant to prove it. On the other side of the road, Great St. Mary's facade and the street of souvenir shops 'sets the scene'–aesthetics have replaced even function.

Masons and other workmen of the period of King's College Chapel

6

The Mystical Purpose

In the middle ages, as before, a church, chapel or
cathedral was not built as a shed, its dimensions determined by the amount of money available, or the size of the
plot upon which it was to be built. Its site was Geomantic-
ally divined for its mystical qualities, and its dimensions
reflect a sacred language, kabbalistically translated into
number, and number into proportion and linear dimension.
King's College Chapel was not just built on a piece of
unoccupied land, available at the time King Henry VI
decided to build it. A church, houses, and the main street
of a prosperous port were demolished in order that the
correct omphalos could be utilized. The closure of the main
street was the cause of a riot as late as 1454. The Flemish
curate of the church, St. John's Zachary, Nicholas Cloos,
was later elevated to a Bishopric. The foundation stone
was laid by the King in person, on an auspicious day, and
was later removed by persons unknown. As the foundation
stone was upon the omphalos, the point where the original

high altar, and perhaps the relics, were (there were relics in the first chapel), so it is probable that the foundation stone was removed when the High Altar was ripped out on the orders of Elizabeth I, the high altar being destroyed. From the site, the projected dimensions, according to the sacred canon of proportion interpreted by the King, were laid out. A sacred temple, the chapel had the rule, which died out in the 1830s, that when a soldier entered wearing spurs, a fine was demanded for profaning God's house.

In 1443, Geomancy in England was at a peak of development. Having been practiced since Megalithic times, Geomantic works contain the same basic sacred geometry. This geometry can be traced thru from Avebury and Stonehenge to Chartres Cathedral and the Church of Our Lady and St. Nicholas in Cambridge. This ancient knowledge was practiced by, among others, the Comacines, Templars, Knights of St. John and Free Masons.

The alinement of churches was, until the Reformation in England, and the Jesuit reaction abroad, east-west. King's College Chapel is alined with an orientation of 6° 20' 3'' north of east. The orientation of the former church of St. John's Zachary, over the sanctuary of which the west end of the chapel was built is unrecorded. However, this need not be the same, as exemplified by the so-called 'deflected chancel' found in numerous churches and cathedrals. This deflected chancel can be found in Cambridge at Great St. Mary's and St. Nicholas, Trumpington. In any case, the chapel represents an eastward extension of the original axis of St. John's Zachary, carrying on the Geomantic alinement laid out centuries before. That God's House had been set up on this site is evidence that it had previous sanctity.

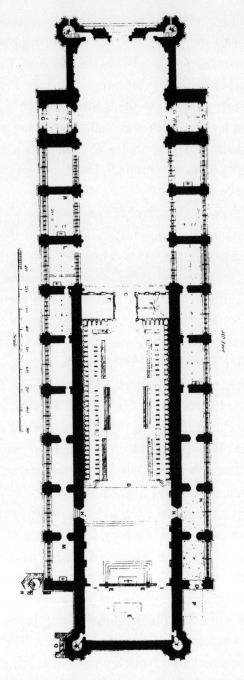

From
'King's College Chapel: Notes on its History and Present Condition'—T.J.P. Carter, 1867

All churches, chapels and cathedrals were oriented, east-west during the pre-reformation period. King's College Chapel is oriented 6° 20' 3" to the North of East. The traditional explanation of orientational deviation is that the buildings were aligned on the sunrise of the day of the Saint to which the church was dedicated. King's College Chapel is dedicated principally to The Virgin Mary, the Moon as opposed to the original foundation of St. John's Zachary, the Sun.

The sun rises at this point of the compass (6° 20' 3" N of E) when its declination is 3° 53' North. At the foundation of the Chapel, the dates when the sun rose at this declination were March 22nd and 4th September. The foundation Stone was laid on 25th July, and the theory of orientation at this time is untenable. According to Sidney Searle's recent researches, much orientation was carried out by the use of the magnetic compass, analogous to the Chinese Geomancers' Compass still used to this day. Magnetic orientation on a scale such as that of King's Chapel, a building of known foundation date, is not possible, as the date the magnetic declination was at this figure was about the year 340, as the orientation of Holy Trinity church at Bosham, Sussex, shows.

Until the sacrosanct King's Lawn is excavated, the possibility of St. John's Zachary having been of Romano-British origin, magnetically oriented, cannot be discounted. If this is the case, the orientation of King's Chapel would have been a continuation of that of St. John's Zachary.

Once the site was cleared, the job of laying out the ground-plan was carried out by Reginald Ely. The 288 feet length was laid out by 12 circles of 12 feet radius. There is good evidence that a module of 4 English feet was used.

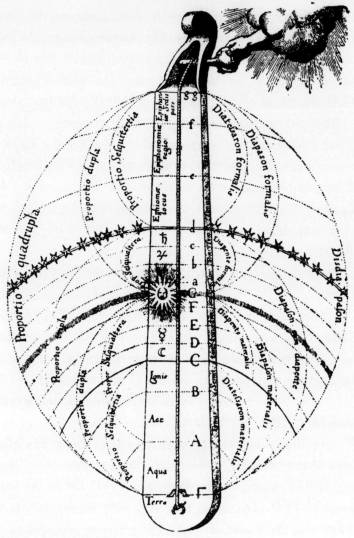

Fludd's Cosmic Harmony compared with the dimensions of King's College Chapel.

Disdiapason   288 feet (12 severies)
Diapason formalis   144 feet (6 severies)
Diapason materialis   144 feet (6 severies)
Diatessaron formalis   96 feet (4 severies)
Diatessaron materialis   96 feet (4 severies)
Diapason cum diapente   192 feet (8 severies)
Diapente formalis   48 feet (2 severies)

Thus the radius of each circle was made out by three modules, making each severy (bay) of six modules (24 feet) by ten modules (40 feet), giving a total ground area of 720 square modules. In modular terms, the ground plan is divided into twelve 5:12:13 integral Pythagorean triangles.

The Freemasons in the Middle Ages. used a device which had been used since antiquity: the Druid's Cord, a rope with twelve knots and thirteen sections. With this tool, it is possible to lay out a right triangle with sections 3:4:5. By practical measurement, and minimal drawing, the ground-plan was laid out, as a concrete application, a living example of number in stone of proportion.

Malden, in 1769 writes, of the masons who built the chapel:

"They have left, I am told, in the cours of their work, certain marks very well known to all adepts of their society. What these monuments of Masonry may be, I am unable to declare; but refer my reader, if he is learned in the secrets of that fraternity, to an inspection of every mysterious token about the building.

One thing, however, I shall mention, which has often been observed,—that in the South Porch of the chapel there are THREE steps, at the west door, FIVE and in the north porch SEVEN. These are numbers, with the mystery or at least with the sound of which Free-Masons are said to be particularly well-acquainted."

The ground plan is composed of 3 pairs of Pythagorean triangles, each 24x10x26 modules. This figure 26 (2x13), is the guiding principle of the building. On the west end, this is expressed in the 1614-15 carving of the tetragrammaton— the Hebrew characters יהוה –JHVH, the secret name of God. In Kabbalistic gematria, the letters J,H,V,H repre-

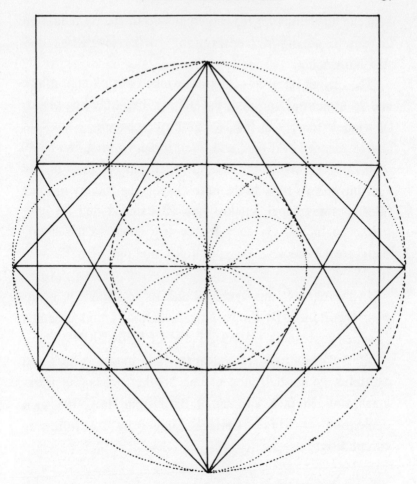

The 24 foot radius inner circle drawn at the junction of two severies is the basis of the interpenetrating equilateral triangles upon which the total width of the chapel is based (84 feet). The equilateral triangle delineates the junction of the third and fourth severy, and a further equilateral triangle projected from the first marks with its base the mid-point of the chapel. The whole length of the chapel is based upon six 24 foot radius circles. The circle circumscribed round the two equilateral triangles (96 feet diameter) delineates the edges of the end towers. Thus the ground plan of King's College Chapel is 'ad triangulum', the Flemish and German system of church construction. The side chapels are each based on a 12 foot radius outer circle with sides based upon inscribed interpenetrating equilateral triangles. See also p. 92, 93.

sent the numbers 10,5,6,5, which add up to 26. By reduction 2 plus 6 equals 8, representing LIFE, ENERGY, and ABUNDANCE.

The chapel itself has 26 great windows of painted glass and 26 structural uprights, but not one free-standing pillar. Of window tracery in the 18 small side-chapels, each side has 13 rounded portions, and 5 rectilinear, giving 26 and 10 respectively. Inside the chapel, each pair of fans in the vaulting has 26 ribs. In the ante-chapel, the tracery of each interior side-chapel window has 12 rounded and 14 long parts, 26 in all. On each of the two doors in the choir, there are 12 crockets (six per side), and one pinnacle −26 in all.

In the chapel, the figure 12 and its multiples is of utmost importance. By Kabbalistic reduction, 1 plus 2 equals 3, which represents HARMONY and PERFECTION.

The conventions of gematria link names which are multiples or submultiples of one another. Thus the tetragrammaton 26 is a version of the Virgin Mary, the main dedication of King's College Chapel by the following calculation:

$$26^2 \quad = \quad 676$$
$$\text{less colel (unity)} \quad = \quad 675$$
$$= \text{'Η ΠΑΡΘΕΝΟΣ ΜΑΡΙΑ}$$

the Virgin Mary

This linkage of numerology and dedication is also expressed in the length of the chapel, as ordered by its founder. The length of the chapel is 288 feet, which equals 192 cubits. 192 is the number of ΜΑΡΙΑΜ. A vesica 192 cubits broad is 332.8 cubits long, numerologically the diagonal of the New Jerusalem. Also 332.8 rounded up to

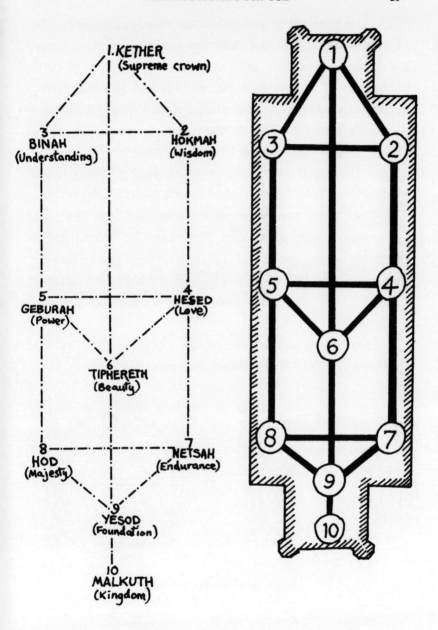

1. KETHER
(Supreme crown)

3
BINAH
(Understanding)

2
HOKMAH
(Wisdom)

5
GEBURAH
(Power)

4
HESED
(Love)

6
TIPHERETH
(Beauty)

8
HOD
(Majesty)

7
NETSAH
(Endurance)

9
YESOD
(Foundation)

10
MALKUTH
(Kingdom)

THE SEPHIROTH AND KING'S CHAPEL

333, is equivalent to half of 666, the mystical number of the Beast of the Apocalypse, also the Number of God.

In feet, the length 288 is equal to the numbers of the 2 sephiroth of the Kabbala Hesed (72) and Gevurah (216), which represent mercy and power. Hesed is masculine and Gevurah feminine, just as the complete dedication is to St. Nicholas (mercy) and Our Lady (power). The combination of Hesed and Gevurah gives forth 'Beauty'— the harmonious balance expressed in the Chapel's proportion. Together these two Sephiroth represent the first two days of creation, and, along with Tiphereth, the Second World, Beri'ah, where reside the Spirits and the highest ranking angels of the Divine hierarchy. The path linking Gevurah and Hesed is number 19–Teth, the Intelligence of Spiritual Activities.

Thus in the dimensions of the chapel is preserved a schema symbolic of its nature and purpose.

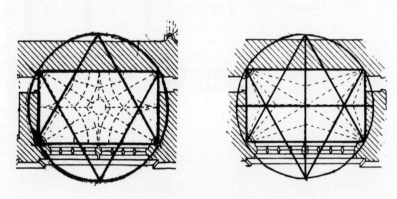

Side-chapel ground geometry

There are 12 severies in the layout of the chapel, each 12 x 2 feet in length, with 4 octagonal corner towers and 22 buttresses, 26 uprights in all. There are 12 great claves, one in the centre of each severy. Above each great side window are 3 quatrefoil lights in square settings—lights to the corridor which runs in the wall above the windows—72 in all (12 x 6).

From these two corridors, 24 entrances (one per severy) allow access to the top of the vaulting, whose thickness at the thinnest part is ½ inch for six inches, according to differing accounts.

The number of fleurons above the small windows and at the ends are 72 plus 12 (84 equals 12x7). Lozenges above the side chantries are 216 (12x18). Fleurons per tower are 8, making 32 in all, whilst fleurons above the side chantries are 108 (12x9). In each end window, there are 18 major panels (called 'days' in the original contract), 36 in all (12x3). Of the intermediate pierced pinnacles on the side walls, there are 36 per side, 72 (12x6) in all. The side windows are 16 (4x4) feet in width, and 49 (7x7) feet high.

The overall length to width ratio of the chapel is very near to the 7:1 ratio discovered by Dr. E.A. Rudge, the Essex antiquary, as common in Saxon churches. The internal length of 288 feet (12x12x 2), by Kabbalistic reduction 2 plus 8 plus 8 equals 18, 1 plus 8 equals 9, the symbol of BROTHERHOOD, the WHOLE BODY OF GOD'S HOUSEHOLD, ORGANIC UNITY. 288 feet is equal to 6.071 Lunar Measures, very close to the diameter across the Aubrey Holes at Stonehenge (eg. the distance between hole 91 and hole 93 across the geometric centre of Stonehenge is 6 LM (1 LM equals 17½ Megalithic Yards; 1 MY equals 2.72 feet). 288 is also integrally close to the ancient Masonic measure of a rod of brickwork, 100 Megalithic Yards, 272 feet, plus one rod (5½ yards). This equals 288½ feet. Also near is 92π feet, 288.2272 feet, and 2½ Roman Actus, 300 Roman feet.

WEST   END

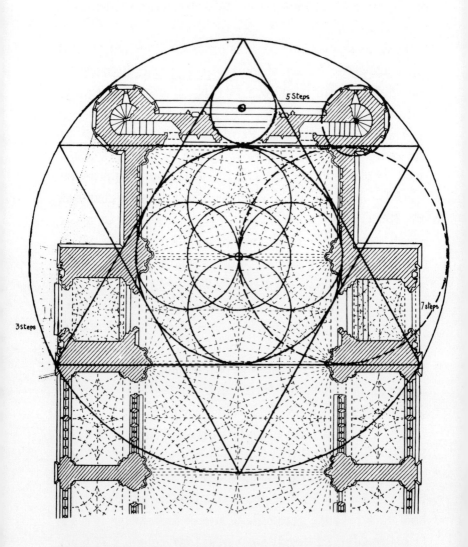

Ground plans of West and East ends of the Chapel showing
geometrical relationships on the system of ad triangulum.
Compare page 87.

EAST END

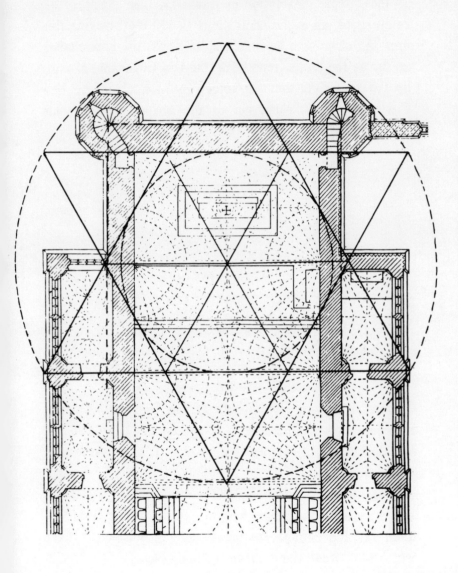

The width of the chapel internally is 40 feet, the same
as the Temple of Solomon in Jerusalem. The length of the
ante-chapel, up to the choir steps is 110 feet, making this
area the same size as the Temple, Thus, the ante-chapel,
as far as the steps, represents the Old Covenant, passing
up the steps and thru the screen into the choir, the New
Covenant. The comparison of the chapel to Solomon's

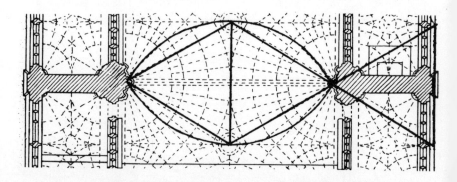

*Equilateral triangles (24 foot sides) show relationship
of springing-point of the vaulting to the external width.*

Temple, which the forerunners of the Freemasons built,
is reminiscent of Justinian's boast, on the completion of
St. Sophia in Constantinople, 537, **"I have surpassed
Solomon."**

The tabernacles flanking the west door have pillars to
support images, the pillars symbolic of the pillars Boaz and
Jachin at the entrance to the Temple of Solomon, pillars
which have great significance in Freemasonry.

The width of the chapel, 40 feet, represents 5x8, LIFE,
8, APPOINTED, 5. The east end contained the stone,
nowadays called the foundation stone, laid at the omphalos
by Henry VI. In the poem by Wolfram von Eschenbach, the

Holy Grail was a stone, and the similar sacred Stone of Destiny lies in the Coronation Chair at Westminster Abbey. These stones originally preserved in their dimensions the ancient metrology, which is expressed in the dimensions of the chapel. Analogous with the Cosmic Cube of the Knights Templar the stone was removed at time unknown. If it was removed at the time of Elizabeth I, it may yet exist somewhere in Cambridge, perhaps incorporated into another building or buried, lest its secrets be destroyed or revealed to non-initiates.

The Geomantic positioning of the chapel is revealed in a local legend. The Manor House of Granchester possesses a massive stone-walled cellar from which issue two passages. One of these extends for a long way, the roof getting lower and lower. It is reputed to run all the way to King's College Chapel, and a fiddler is supposed to have entered the tunnel in search of its end, playing loudly. The music faded as he got further from the entrance, finally to stop. The fiddler was never seen again. This passage has never been investigated from the King's end. It would have to pass beneath the river to get to Granchester. However, it may follow an ancient alinement, as discovered by Alfred Watkins, the Hereford antiquary, in his researches into the alinements of ancient sites.

This was the last temple in England to be built entirely to the Geomantic schemata, handed down from antiquity as the Cosmic Measure—a scheme uniting Man with the Macrocosmos, carefully executed in the correct manner, overriding politics, civil war and dynastic changes.

The perpendicular form of gothic originated in the Court School of Masons, who built Old St. Paul's chapter house in the form in 1332. It is an expression of the spiritual made physical, the manifestation in stone and glass of the arcane schema which governs the cosmos, subservient alone to the Will of God. This contrasts most markedly with the Renaissance's neo-classical, a massiveness derived from the military materialism of Imperialist Rome, a massiveness contrived to crush the spirit of Man into the service of the all-important State Machine. In the Gothic, Man is freed from wordly ordinances to strive for higher planes of being thru the action of an instrument of trans-mutation—in this case, the chapel. In the neo-classical

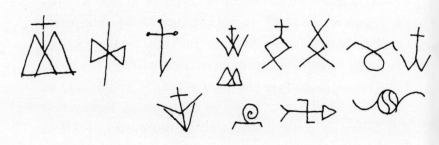

Ante-chapel pre 1515

Side Chapels, pre 1461

Other chantries

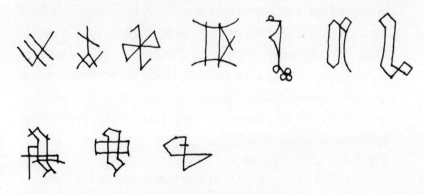

Other chantries pre 1515

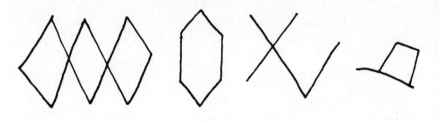

signed 'Richard Morris'   *Upper surface main vaulting (Wastell)*

Gatehouse of old court, pre 1461

(itself a 'loaded' term) the essential unity of Man and creation, microcosm and macrocosm as part of the same Universal scheme, is destroyed, and 'art' and 'architecture' become formalized into the products of academies—judged solely on the grounds of aesthetic acceptability within the framework of 'permitted' styles. Such an attitude is all-pervasive today, when angular concrete is all that is permitted as architectural. Ceasing to be naturally based on a universal metrological system, architecture became, after the untimely demise of Gothic, a succession of fashionable styles, more or less based on permutations of antique themes, devices and motifs, until the organic secession of Art Nouveau, and finally the puritanical baldness of the Modern Style, imposed by both the academic world and economic theory.

As the religious aspect of life faded, due to the Reformation, the chapel was reaching completion. It was never finished, as it belonged to quite a different world from the post-Reformation one. The ritual had changed, obviating the need for 17 altars. The chantries had been suppressed, so no more prayers were offered for the souls of the departed. The colour intended was absent, and, as years passed, the vestments were abolished, the language was changed from Latin to English, the incense was stopped, the music altered, then removed, altars were smashed and re-erected. John Frith and Laurence Sanders were burnt for religious offences, as were Robert Glover and John Hullier, the latter burnt on Jesus Green in Cambridge, during Mary's reign, for writing a tract on the Common-Prayer. All were from King's College.

As the effects of Religion were destroyed, so financiers, usurers and bankers became increasingly important. No longer were Christians forbidden to lend money, and economic considerations of space caused expedient designs to be adopted, without regard to Geomancy. Master Masons, such as John Rogers, became military engineers. Orientation of churches was deliberately defied, as at Sir Walter Mildmay's puritan Emmanuel College, 1584, where he converted the hall, oriented north-south, into the chapel, and the chapel, oriented east-west, into the hall.

Geomancy was dismissed as 'superstition'. After the Reformation, sacred architecture was abandoned. Henry Wotton, in Elements of Architecture, 1624, writes on gothic architecture:

"This form, both for the natural imbecility of the sharp angle itself, and likewise for its very Uncomelinesse, ought to be exiled from judicious eyes, and left to its first inventors, the Gothes and Lombardes, among other Reliques of that barbarous age."

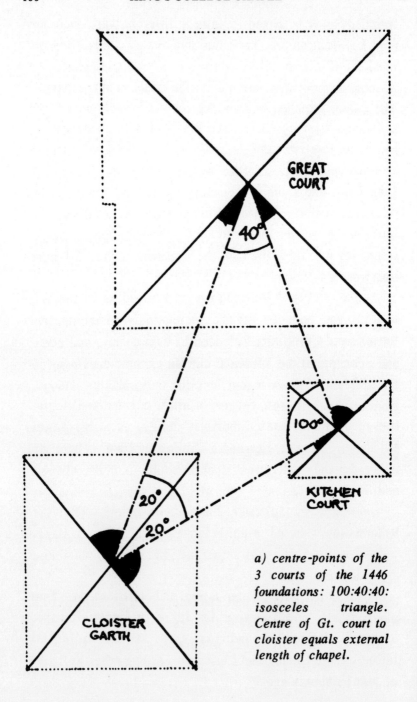

a) centre-points of the 3 courts of the 1446 foundations: 100:40:40: isosceles triangle. Centre of Gt. court to cloister equals external length of chapel.

King's College Chapel, despite its sacred canonical dimensions, became a spectacle, no longer recognized as a unique instrument for enlightenment. During the lengthy construction, the original plans were rigidly adhered to, under the Ninth Article of Masonry, from the Articles and Points of Masonry, fourteenth century:

"The ninth article is this, that no master shall supplant another, for it is said that in the art of masonry that no man can bring to an end so well the work begun by another to the profit of his Lord as he that began it, unless it be by his designs or by him to whom he shows his designs."

When the masons left off, 'art' took over, and Renaissance woodwork crammed with alien pagan irrelevencies, and the whole sad tale of altars erected only to be abolished. The principle of the Temple as the Microcosm, the Universe as the Macrocosm, was lost, and the 'picturesque' and the 'curious' emerged as a concept. Buildings were demolished in front of the chapel, and vistas, bearing no relationship to spirituality, were opened up. Lack of funds prevented the realization of the rest of the scheme. The original moneys had come thru the seizure of cells of foreign Abbeys under the authority of a Papal Bull of January 31st 1448/9, but, with the Wars of the Roses, the miserliness, until old age, of Henry VII, and the futile expense of defending Boulogne during the reign of Henry VIII, thwarted the scheme until times had changed, and the significance was forgotten, or considered unnecessary.

By the time Toft Monks wood was cut down, the neo-classical was in use. The cemetery, which had been the churchyard of St. John's Zachary, had become part of 'the

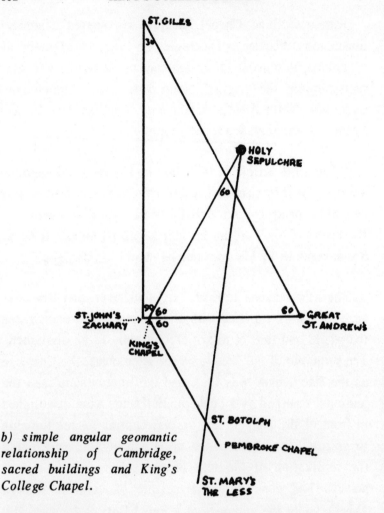

b) simple angular geomantic relationship of Cambridge, sacred buildings and King's College Chapel.

Backs', a bowling green, and is now part of what is known as King's Lawn.

Today (as since the eighteenth century) the attitude to the chapel is in terms of 'art'. Fuller wrote of the chapel as:

"**one of the rarest fabricks in Christendom, wherein the stonework, woodwork and glasswork contend which shall deserve most admiration. Yet the first generally carrieth**

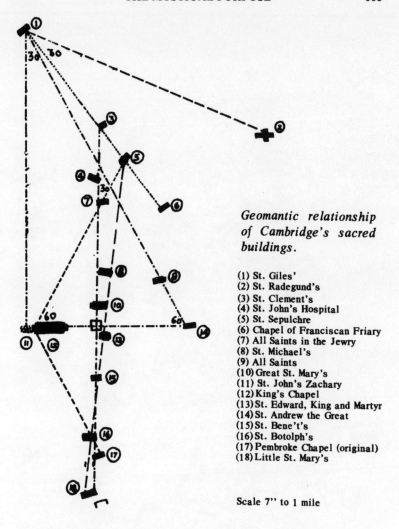

Geomantic relationship of Cambridge's sacred buildings.

(1) St. Giles'
(2) St. Radegund's
(3) St. Clement's
(4) St. John's Hospital
(5) St. Sepulchre
(6) Chapel of Franciscan Friary
(7) All Saints in the Jewry
(8) St. Michael's
(9) All Saints
(10) Great St. Mary's
(11) St. John's Zachary
(12) King's Chapel
(13) St. Edward, King and Martyr
(14) St. Andrew the Great
(15) St. Bene't's
(16) St. Botolph's
(17) Pembroke Chapel (original)
(18) Little St. Mary's

Scale 7" to 1 mile

away the credit, (as being a stone henge indeed) so geometrically contrived, that voluminous stones mutually
support themselves in the arched roof, as if art had made
them forget nature, and weaned them of their fondness to
descend to their center. And yet, though there be so much
of Minerva, there is nothing of Arachne in this building: I
mean not a spider appearing...........''

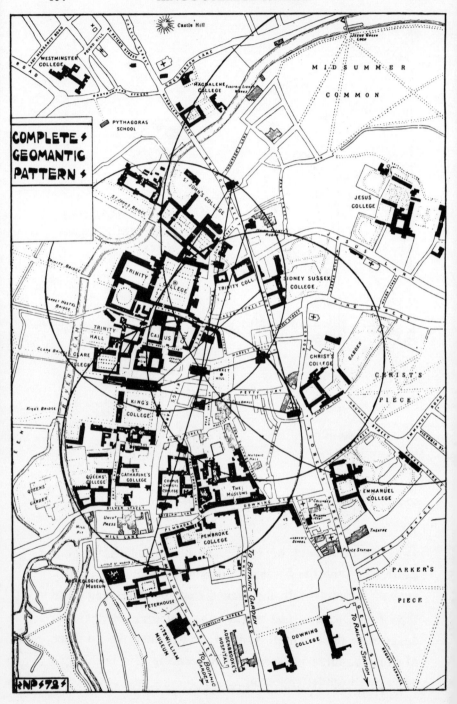

John Proctor Carter, in his 1867 history of the Chapel, wrote:

"It is entitled to be ranked with the finest buildings of the world."

The 'Aesthetic', Ruskin was very severe, comparing it to a billiard table turned upside down—a symptom of the total lack of understanding which had been reached by his era, and which scarcely relaxes its grip today.

This attitude had enabled the destruction of the east end's occult significance, by the demolition of the steps, to occur within the last ten years. In this last act, the ancient brickwork was found to rest on the soil—directly in contact with the telluric energies—before it was shattered by pneumatic drills in order to erect a steel frame to support a painting in a fake tryptych, a gift too valuable to be refused.

What has been done to the chapel since the time of Henry VIII represents an abject failure to comprehend the religious significance of this, the final flowering of the Great Work.

Afterword

King's College Chapel is still a unique structure. A royal foundation in a city, which, for Geomantic reasons, was the home of many Monastic orders, it was continued as a religious duty by the Kings who succeeded the founder. Because of the Reformation and the Renaissance, it was never finished, and remains unpainted, without stone screen, images or altars. However, the finest craftsmen in the land were used on the chapel, and this is undoubtedly the reason why it is held in such awe even to this day. Another reason is that, altho mutilated and misused, it still retains the sanctity inherent in its dimensions, siting and orientation, its atmosphere a living proof of the arts of the Geomancer and the Mason. To quote Hermon G. Wood (**Ideal Metrology, 1908**) "**.....It is a wonderful product of human skill, inspired thruout with profound and ceaseless reverence for Nature's ideal of harmony, the human and the Divine working together to realize that which is beyond the reach of individual effort.**"

Appendix One
Vitruvianism

At the Reformation, the ancient Gothic lore of the freemasons was suppressed. This culminated in the deliberate mis-orientation of ecclesiastical buildings, such as the chapel of Emmanuel College in Cambridge set up in 1584 by Sir Walter Mildmay. This chapel, however, was never consecrated, but replaced, on the orders of the master, William Sancroft (who became dean of St. Paul's Cathedral, 1664). Built by the freemasons Simon Wise and Nicholas Ashby, the chapel was designed by Sir Christopher Wren and orientated correctly. Wren is considered the greatest English Renaissance architect, his masterpiece St. Paul's, the first Protestant cathedral. The theoretical writings of the August-an Roman, Vitruvius, were consciously or unconsciously the basis of the Renaissance style of architecture. Both Palladio and Alberti acknowledge Vitruvius as their mentor and we find a proliferation of tributes to his ideas amongst the theoreticians and architects who created the new age of architecture. Thus Luca Pacioli's *'De Divina Proportione'*, illustrated by diagrams drawn by his friend Leonardo da Vinci, discussed in Vitruvian terms the divine proportions, the central idea of Renaissance philosophy.

Pacioli's book was amongst the library of Dr. John Dee, the famous Elizabethan Magus who was responsible for introducing, and popularizing, Vitruvianism into England. In 1570, the same year in which Palladio published his *'bible'*, Dr. Dee published a new edition of Euclid, to which he wrote a lengthy preface. This preface, based on Vitruvius, expounds the Renaissance concept of the architect, with long quotations from Vitruvius and Alberti. It is important to note that, with the exception of the lengthy quotes in Dee's preface, no English translation of Alberti was available in England until the eighteenth century. The preface opens with a general Pythagorean-Platonic mystical discussion of number, continuing with an enumeration of the sciences dealing with number, which are arithmetic, algebra and geometry. Dee deals with the sciences, showing their dependence on number. Dee's sciences are the Vitruvian subjects: Number and calculation, music, land measurement, painting and drawing of proportion and perspective, military art, motions and machinery, time measurement, cosmography and geography, astrology—all of which are subservient to architecture. Dee refers his readers to Book 1, Chapter 3, which discusses the design of temples, which, says Vitruvius, depends on the symmetry and proportion of the human body which are to be reflected in the symmetry and proportion of the temple.

The geometry of the square and circle, with the analogies implied by Vitruvius, became the guiding principle in the construction of Renaissance round churches, such as Donato Bramante's Tempietto at St. Pietro, Montorio, Rome, built on the site where St. Peter was crucified. Dee gives two other references for the geometry of the square and circle as basic for the theory of proportion: Durer and Agrippa. With Agrippa, we are back again with Vitruvius, but with the addition of astrology and magic. Thus to the Vitruvian man, Agrippa adds the characters of the signs of the zodiac and the planets, also the idea of the harmony of the soul and of the effects of music in harmonizing it with the universe. Here, as in Gothic architecture, we have the reflection of cosmic and human proportions in basic geometrical terms—which for Fludd was the expression of microcosm and macrocosm. Thus the divine temple expressed in numerical and geometrical terms the map of the heavens, the motion of the planets, the calendar, the zodiac, and man himself.

This mystical mathematics, based on Vitruvius, was reflected in another great Renaissance architect, Juan Herrera, the favourite architect of King Philip II of Spain, who helped design the Escorial. Both the king and Herrera were deeply involved in

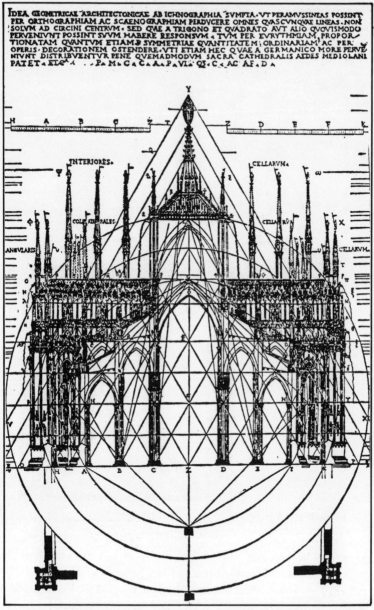

Section of Milan Cathedral, from Cesare Cesariano's 1521 edition of Vitruvius, showing the German 'ad triangulum' system of proportion employed for the design of the cathedral, the system used for the ground-plan of King's College Chapel.

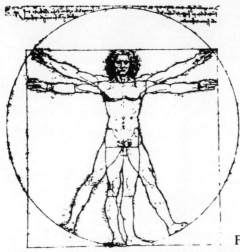

From L. da Vinci

From H.C. Agrippa

astrology and magic, were ardent Lullists and collectors of the works of Hermes Trismegistus and his followers. The Escorial's proportions and design are based upon the Jesuit Villalpanda's works on the Vision of Ezekiel and his reconstruction of the Temple of Solomon. Herrera was an avowed Vitruvian. Dr. Yates considers that *"Herrera and Dee (and Fludd) represent a stage of Renaissance Vitruvianism at which the growing strength of the Hermetic influence turns Vitruvius himself into a Magus and infuses magical and cosmological overtones into the proportions of Vitruvian Man".*

Along with Dee, the other English Vitruvian was the Jacobean, Robert Fludd of Oxford University. There is more than a direct link between Fludd's mnemonic diagrams and Leonardo da Vinci's diagrams—both men were consciously illustrating the identical theory—Vitruvianism. With the exception of playhouses

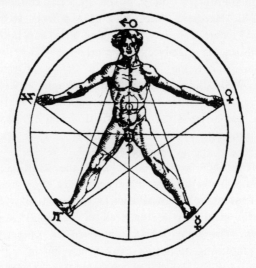

From Fludd.

consciously Vitruvian architecture was not constructed in England until the 1620s by the *'Vitruvius Britannicus'*—Inigo Jones, the grand architect to the court of King Charles I. Inigo Jones was the first person to publish the underlying schema of Stonehenge (as he saw it), a Vitruvian design. Jones' grand designs were delayed by the revolution which overthrew both king and court, and by the unthinkable idea of destroying a whole city, starting again from scratch. This unprecedented opportunity was presented after the Great Fire of London destroyed much of the capital in 1666. Thus the architects were given an unparalleled opportunity to design a whole new city. Wren prepared a plan, but property interests caused its abandonment. Neither Inigo Jones nor Sir Christopher Wren would ever have had the license allowed to modern architects who regard it as commonplace to raze and rebuild whole city centres.

Inigo Jones had been 'architect' in charge of a piecemeal rebuilding of Old St. Paul's, which had suffered a fire and fallen into disrepair. To this end, he built a Vitruvian facade at the West-end (1633). When the cathedral was burnt, along with much of London, Sir Christopher Wren, who had been toying with the idea of demolishing it, decided to build a completely new edifice. The present building, tho Renaissance in detail, is built according to Gothic principles, based upon Ely Cathedral, where Wren's uncle, Matthew Wren, was bishop from 1638 to 1667 (including 17 years in prison). Matthew Wren had built the last Gothic building in Cambridge, Peterhouse Chapel (1628-32), George Thompson being freemason in charge of the building. Christopher Wren studied the celebrated octagon at Ely, the only Gothic dome, designed by Alan of Walsingham and William Hurley in 1328-40, and utilized the same principles in his design of the St. Paul's crossing which supports the brick cone which is the structural core of the wooden outer dome.

Wren went once a year to look at the vaulting of King's College Chapel, saying that if anyone could show him where to place the first stone, he would build another like it. St. Paul's cathedral was originally designed as an octagonal church with a longer nave. The final design, approved by King Charles II, himself a practising alchemist, was a merging of Vitruvian and Gothic principles. St. Paul's has an aisled nave, aisled transepts, an aisled choir and a clerestory, all similar to Ely Cathedral, which is just seventeen feet longer. The Gothic constructional system is most apparent in the flying buttresses, which are concealed by the external screen wall. Wren himself said that he used the old *"Cathedral Form"*, rectified *"as to reconcile the Gothick to a better form of Architecture"*. Thus, with Wren the Vitruvian principles of the Renaissance and the Gothic masonic secrets of Ely and King's College Chapel were synsethized. Wren himself was master of an operative lodge of freemasons, who, under Mr. Strong, were employed in the construction of the last of the old cathedrals. St Paul's reflects the ancient canonical lore in its dimensions. The height is 365 feet, equivalent to the number of days in a year. In length, 500 feet, it equals the length of a vesica whose width is the length of King's College Chapel. The length in cubits is the number of the diagonal of the New Jerusalem. The whole ground-plan is based on a double square.

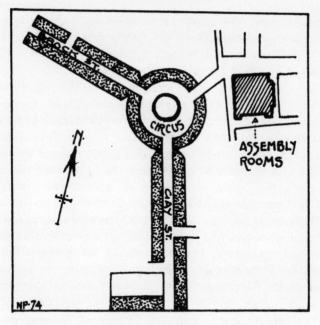

Plan of the Circus and associated streets in Bath,
designed 1725, (the year Inigo Jones 'Stonehenge'
was re-published), based upon the proportions of
Stonehenge by John Wood.

Wren is considered one of the greatest English architects. The
Great Architect, an idea taken from Vitruvius, leads without
difficulty to the Great Architect of the Universe of masonry or
the Divine Mathematician of Newtonism. Therefore it is not
surprising to find that Isaac Newton, the father of modern Science,
was also a founder member of the new Masonic Order, a Rosicrucian, and a lifelong practising, if secret, alchemist. This is apart
from his heretical religious beliefs.

Thus Science, the exterminator of superstition and the super-
natural, simultaneously gave birth to its counterpart, which
related directly to the age-old canonical law. It is an important
fact that Inigo Jones found his quintessential Vitruvian temple in
Stonehenge, indeed was so taken with its ability to fit Vitruvianism that he declared that it must be of Roman origin since no
druids could have had sufficient knowledge of Vitruvianism. A
later architect who took Stonehenge as his inspiration was John
Wood, Jr., who designed Royal Crescent in Bath, patterning his

colonnades upon the megalithic proportions, and the approach street upon the Avenue. Wren was finally dismissed as architect of St. Paul's when a committee forced him to either accept a change or go. This change was the addition of a balustrade to the top of the external screen wall, destroying the proportion.

The Vitruvian/Gothic synthesis was utilized by several Continental Baroque architects in their ground-plans and facades. Giovanni Santini (1667-1723), member of a family of Italian freemasons, constructed churches in a gothic-baroque synthesis. At Zd'ar, in Moravia, he constructed the *'pilgrimage church on the green hill'* on a ground-plan of a pentagram, with five additional pentagonal chapels, a church which, in certain ways, foreshadows art nouveau. Born in 1687, Balthasar Neumann (who used reinforced concrete for his vaulting) was trained as a civil and military engineer, becoming one of the greatest Baroque architects. Certain of his churches, especially the pilgrimage church of the Vierzehnheiligen, in West Germany, however, are gothic in facade proportions, showing the continuing arcane tradition which began with the Temple of Solomon and the Pyramid of Zoser at Saqqara (designed by Imhotep).

Appendix Two

Independent Observations on the Chapel's Metrology

Michael Behrend, the Cambridge metrologist, has discovered the following correspondences of metrological units in the dimensions of the ground-plan of the chapel:-

The chapel conforms to a square grid in which each square has a side of *3x* the postulated basic unit *H* of *70cm*. This unit *H* corresponds to *1/420 Th* of the basic landscape geometry unit *X* discovered by Mr. Behrend.

According to this system:

Length of North and South porches	*- 6H - 4.2 metres*
Length of side chapels	*- 9H - 6.3 metres*
Partition between side chapels	*- 1.5H - 1.05 metres*
Interval between vaults	*- 10.5H - 7.35 metres*

The total external length of the chapel is *138H*.

138 - 6 x 23, multiples of *23* units occuring frequently in the landscape geometry of the Cambridge region, notably in connexion with Shonke's Moat on the Virgo figure in the Nuthampstead Zodiac.

The total external width of the chapel	*- 37H*
Length of East part (chapel proper)	*- 74H*
Internal width of the East part	*- 18.5H*

These numbers are in the simple ratio: *2:4:1* and are also exact factors of *666*, identified by the noted cosmologist John Michell as a solar number! The length of the antechapel is *54H*, *54* being an exact factor of the lunar number *1080*.

RECOMMENDED FURTHER READING

T.J.P. Carter "King's College Chapel: Notes on its History and present Condition" *Macmillan 1867*

L. Charpentier "The Mysteries of Chartres Cathedral" *R.I.L.K.O. 1972*

E.J. Eitel "Feng-Shui. Natural Science in China" *Cokaygne 1973*

Fulcanelli "The Mysteries of the Cathedrals" *Neville Spearman 1971*

J. Heinsch "Grundsatze vorzeitliche Kultgeographie" (Principles of Prehistoric Sacred Geography) *Comptes Rendus du Congres International de Geographie 1938*

G. Lesser "Gothic Cathedrals and Sacred Geometry" *Alec Tiranti 1957*

J. Michell "City of Revelation" *Abacus 1973*

J.F. Newton "The Builders" *Allen and Unwin 1962*

N. Pennick "Geomancy" *Cokaygne 1973*

W. Shakespeare "King Henry VI" parts I and II

W. Stirling "The Canon" *Garnstone Press 1974*

F.C. Tyler "The Geometrical Arrangement of Ancient Sites" *Simpkin Marshall 1939*

Vitruvius (trans. M.H. Morgan) "The Ten Books on Architecture" *Dover 1960*

H.G. Wood "Ideal Metrology in Nature, Art, Religion and History" *Privately Published Dorchester, Massachusetts, 1908*

F. Yates "The Theatre of the World" *Routledge and Kegan Paul 1969*

Index

F

D

G

E

T

U

V

W

"Who is able to build Him an house, seeing the heaven and heaven of
heavens cannot contain Him? who am I then, that I should build
Him an house, save only to burn sacrifice before Him?
"Send me now therefore a man cunning to work in gold, and
in silver, and in brass, and in iron, and in purple, and
crimson, and blue, and that can skill to grave with the
cunning men that are with me in Judah and in Jerusalem, whom David my father did provide. Send
me also cedar-trees, fir-trees, and algum-trees,
out of Lebanon: for I know that thy servants can skill to cut timber in Lebanon;
and, behold, my servants shall be
with thy servants, even to prepare
me timber in abundance :
for   the   house   which
I am about to build
shall be great and
wonderful." —
2 Chron. ii.
6—9.

✠